EASTERN TEXAS HISTORY

EASTERN TEXAS HISTORY

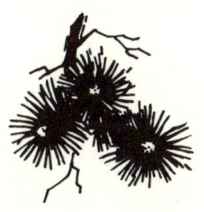

Selections from the East Texas Historical Journal

Edited by
Archie P. McDonald

Jenkins Publishing Company
Austin, Texas/1978

COPYRIGHT © 1978

JENKINS BOOK PUBLISHING COMPANY, INC.
BOX 2085, AUSTIN, TEXAS 78768
ALL RIGHTS RESERVED

DESIGNED BY
LARRY SMITHERMAN

LIBRARY OF CONGRESS CATALOG NO. 78-62318
I.S.B.N. 0-8363-0159-5

CONTENTS

    Introduction, by Archie McDonald 7
1. The Penetration of Foreigners and Foreign Ideas into Spanish East Texas, by Odie B. Faulk 11
2. LaSalle and the Historians, by Ert. J. Gum 29
3. McMahan's Chapel: Landmark in Texas, by Walter N. Vernon 43
4. The Elusive East Texas Border, by Thomas F. Ruffin 55
5. "River People," by William Seale 81
6. East Texas in the Election of 1860, and the Secession Crisis, by Allan C. Ashcraft 95
7. Life in Civil War East Texas, by Ralph A. Wooster 111
8. Black Texans during Reconstruction: First Freedom, by James Smallwood 127
9. The Pines of Texas, a Study in Lumbering and Public Policy, 1880-1930, by Robert S. Maxwell 151

10. Just a Few Childhood Memories of
    Mattie Dupree Steussy, edited by
    Robert W. Shook 169
11. Margie E. Neal: First Woman Senator
    in Texas, by Walter L. Harris 183
12. Bride of the Forest, by Ava Bush 201
13. Historical Aspects of Linguistic Research
    in East Texas, by Fred A. Tarpley 211
14. The World's Champion Fiddlers'
    Festival at Crockett: An East Texas
    Tradition, by Joe Angle 225

Introduction

A news story should include for its readers the essential who, what, where, when and why of the thing. Novels demand plots with finely etched characters, settings, and sequence. Narrative history and biography need structure, direction, selectivity of data and interpretation. An anthology, which is what this book about East Texas is supposed to be, is simply a collection of literary works; it is blank verse, impressionistic painting, "modern" art, and "progressive" music in words, pictures, and charts.

Yet those things which characterize a good news story, a novel, or a narrative history are all combined here in a potpourri of East Texana. The "who" is the cumulative and conglomerative interaction of three centuries of Indian, Spanish, Mexican, Anglo, European, African, and Oriental migration. The "what" is the results of their mutual experiences. The "where" is west of the Sabine River, south of the Red River, east of the Trinity River, and north of the Gulf of Mexico. The "when" is from Genesis till now, and the "why" is still one of the puzzles the Lord is letting us try to figure out. We have our established characters, our setting, and our sequence as well as the rest of the qualifiers. Still, it is difficult to be definitive about East Texas. Boundaries are established, the people are stereotyped, politics are predictable, the economy is diverse and healthy, but ask a native or an outsider to **define** East Texas and you are likely to produce confusion.

There are some folks who react as they think they are expected to react: "outsiders" condescend, condemn, or overcompensate; "insiders" condone, grow defensive, or boast. One sure way to tell which group you are dealing with is to listen to the drawl and see the way they write "East": if they sound the "T" deliberately or fail to capitalize the "E," you know you are dealing with a foreigner. Their kind probably thinks of East Texas as prejudiced, countrified, backward. The others are likely to feel that their section of the state is picked on, really progressive, and if not perfect, at least it tries hard.

Well, I **said** it is difficult to define. The fact is, it is even more difficult to gain much perspective on the subject if you start out your earthly days, as I did, as an East Texan. You never get much choice in the matter; if this is your beginning, it is likely to be your life's home. Oh, we have our Van Cliburns and Y. A. Tittles and William Owenses who go away and make something of themselves, but even they usually come back. It's home, and maybe that's enough said.

The East Texas discussed and analyzed in these thirteen selections stretches the river boundaries and sprawls across the centuries. It is beautiful or ugly depending on the topic being discussed and on the bias or the prejudice of the reader as well as the writer. Its range is broad. East Texas extends from the Gulf coastal prairies to the rolling red-dirt hills and on to the black land of the northwest section, from the semi-urbanities of Beaumont, Tyler-Longview, and Texarkana to the gravy-soppers of the Big Thicket and the pea-pickers of Athens, and from Spanish explorers to Anglo river captains and lumber barons.

These essays and articles were authored by a diverse group. Some are professional historians. Others would shudder in fear they might be classed as such. Some live and work in the region, others are scattered as far away as Omaha and Washington, D. C. All have competence in the area on which they have written. Odie B. Faulk's article on borderlands encounters between Spaniards and Anglos is one of many articles and books to his credit. Ert Gum is a knowledgeable French historian who has handled the still controversial career of La Salle controversially. Walter N. Vernon knows as much about Texas religious history as anyone, and he writes here about McMahan's Chapel. Tom Ruffin is from Louisiana because he couldn't solve the boundary dispute he writes about so well to include himself in East Texas. William Seale's river people are captured with affection. Allan Ashcraft, Ralph Wooster, and James Smallwood, three distinguished historians, bring life and meaning to the complicated but extremely crucial period of secession-war-reconstruction. Robert Shook's edition of Mattie Dupree Steussy's folksy reminiscenses make us misty-eyed for a by-gone day but glad we do not have the same hardships. Walter Harris' "Margie Neal" suggests that women have been important in Texas politics all along. Ava Bush's tribute to the dogwood reminds us that Robert S. Maxwell's woodsmen spared one of the prettiest of the forest's offerings. Fred Tarpley amuses and informs us about our colloquialisms while Joe Angle makes our foot pat with his article on the old time fiddlers.

This is a diverse group, but there is a common denominator. All of these articles have previously appeared in the **East Texas Historical Journal**, which has been in business since 1963. Some of them were published near the beginning, others are gathered from along the way to the latest volume.

The **Journal** is sponsored by the East Texas Historical Association, and is headquartered at Stephen F. Austin State University. The **Journal**'s first editor, a co-founder of the Association, and an inspiration of much of the modern study of East Texas history was Charles

K. ("Dick") Chamberlain. Other founders and early workers included Ralph W. Steen, Lee Lawrence, Mrs. Tommie Jan Lowery, and F. I. Tucker. When Dr. Chamberlain retired in 1972, I was asked to become editor on a probationary basis and since nothing has been said since then I suppose it is working out. I am proud of the articles which I helped edit and thankful for those Dr. Chamberlain prepared for publication. Maybe together they will capture some of the sounds and smells and sights and meanings of our past and make us more aware of our East Texas.

Archie P. McDonald
Editor
Nacogdoches, Texas

1

THE PENETRATION OF FOREIGNERS AND FOREIGN IDEAS INTO SPANISH EAST TEXAS

by
Odie B. Faulk

Odie B. Faulk is Chairman of the Department of History at Oklahoma State University, Stillwater, Oklahoma. He is the author of many historical studies, including **North America Divided.**

1

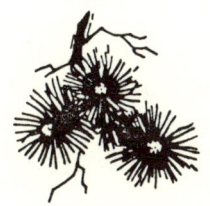

A backwater to the mainstream of world politics, the Eastern Interior Provinces of New Spain[1] (Coahuila, Nuevo Leon, Nuevo Santander, and Texas) nevertheless felt the impact of the French Revolution and the period of wars and intrigue that followed. Spanish officials in these provinces — commandants-general, governors, and army officers — for the most part were loyal adherents to the centuries-old royal tradition, and were determined to stop the spread of the doctrines of liberty, equality, and fraternity. Even before this period, in fact, they were suspicious and fearful of foreigners and foreign ideas. Their suspicion stemmed from provincialism, religious nationalism, and past events. Their fear was grounded in military weakness: the number of Spaniards in these provinces was few, especially in Texas, compared to the tens of thousands of fickle natives surrounding them. Therefore, following the outbreak of war in Europe in early 1793, these officials redoubled their efforts to keep foreign agents away from the Indians, as well as to keep foreign ideas away from their own people.

In the fall of 1793 when official confirmation arrived that Spain had joined with England and other European nations in a war against France, there was an immediate increase in tensions in the Eastern Interior Provinces. From Chihuahua City Commandant-General Pedro de Nava[2] in November sent instructions to Governor Manuel Muñoz of Texas[3] to dispatch an armed expedition to the Gulf Coast area. The leader of this party was to exhort the Indians not to treat with any French landing party, and he was to promise rich rewards to the chiefs if they would relay quickly the news of any French activities to Spanish officials.[4] When rumors reached San Antonio a few months later that French agents were working among the tribes of North Texas, Nava likewise ordered an expedition to that region.[5]

Viceroy Miguel de la Grua Talamanca y Branciforte (1794-1798) was not content that sufficient precautions had been taken in Nava's area of command. In December he ordered that all Frenchmen in the Eastern Interior Provinces be arrested and confined. However, Texas was exempted from the provisions of this decree because of the large number of Louisiana-born French living there.[6] Such practices ceased in July of the following year when word arrived from Europe that peace had been re-established with France.[7]

Nevertheless, Spanish officials remained zealous in their efforts to prevent the entry into the area of French revolutionary doctrines in the form of printed matter. As quickly as such works became known, they were banned by the government and placed on the church list of proscribed works. For example, in November of 1794 Nava ordered the governors under his command to seize all copies of **The Disenchantment of Man**, a work printed in Spanish in Philadelphia. All copies of the book were to be confiscated, and all persons arrested who possessed it or had read it.[8] In October of the following year came a similar order regarding a manuscript entitled, "Discourse pronounced by Boisi d'Anglas, Member of the Public Order. . . ." Nava concluded his dispatch with the prophetic words: "Exercise care about the types of material in circulation, for by this manner our religion, king, state, cult, vassalage, and security may be lost."[9]

The war with France was hardly ended before another source of worry arose to replace it. In October of 1796 Nava informed his governors that the English were counterfeiting Spanish pesos at Birmingham, England, with the intention of introducing them into the New World to wreck the economy in the colonies.[10] Within four months came word that war had been declared against England;[11] and with this news there was a wave of fear, amounting almost to hysteria, that the English and Americans were planning a joint invasion of Louisiana, and possibly Texas. Governor Muñoz wrote his superior that he had taken all possible precautions to meet the threat: frequent inspections of the coast had been ordered, and diligent efforts were being made to keep enemy agents from going among the Indians.[12]

The fear that the United States might invade the Eastern Interior Provinces was not new in 1797. In fact, such a feeling had been growing since the signing three years earlier of the treaty between the United States and England (Jay's Treaty). To the Spaniards this accord seemed a prelude to aggression. And as in the case of the French, there soon were rumors that American agents were circulating among the Indian tribes in Texas.[13]

On July 30, 1795, Nava wrote Governor Muñoz of Texas that "the king has been informed on good authority that the United States has ordered emissaries to move here [Interior Provinces] and work to subvert the population." He noted that dispatches from the Baron de Carondelet, Governor of Louisiana, told of "greedy persons from the western states" moving into the interior of that province. He concluded with a warning to "exercise care to see that no foreigners go among the Indian nations that are our allies."[14] Even news of the signing of a treaty between Spain and the United States (Pinckney's Treaty) did not allay suspicions of American aggression in the Interior Provinces.[15]

Despite the fact that no invasion ever materialized and no enemy agents were caught, the tension continued to mount among Spanish officials. As France and Spain had allied in the European struggle, and as an undeclared war was raging between France and the United States in the late 1790's, the commanding-general feared that Americans might attempt a sudden seizure of Spanish territory. Especially alarming to this official was the granting by Congress of authority for President John Adams to raise an army of ten thousand men. In August of 1798 Nava wrote Muñoz, ". . . some feel that [the Americans] shortly will declare hostilites with us. In view of this, you are to take all precautions to put the province under your command in a good state of defense."[16] Two months later he wrote that the quarrel between the United States and France made "an outbreak of war almost inevitable."[17]

The victim of this Spanish fear of the United States was Philip Nolan. This enigmatic figure first came to Texas as early as 1785, professing to be a horse trader.[18] In 1794-1795 he made another trip to the province, visiting at San Antonio and La Bahía (present Goliad) to purchase horses for the Spanish governor of Louisiana.[19] In the fall of 1797 Nolan returned, this time with permission to travel to Nuevo Santander on a passport signed by Commandant-General Nava.[20] Before this trip was completed, however, Nolan's fall from favor had begun. Nava revoked Nolan's permit to import two thousand pesos worth of goods to be used as presents for friendly Indians, giving "good reasons" as the grounds for his action.[21] When the horse trader remained in Texas an additional year for vague reasons, the commandant-general became very suspicious. In April of 1799 Nava wrote the governor of Texas: "Tell me if in your opinion he has made himself suspect; but, in truth, to me his residing here so long has not seemed good when less time would have been sufficient to gather the horses I permitted. . . ."[22]

Muñoz answered the request for information by stating: "In examining [Nolan's] conduct, I find that he never did anything suspicious. . . . Always he has manifested much affection and gratitude for our government. . . ."[23] This reply did little to restore Nava's shaken confidence in the American, and in June of 1799 he ordered the horse trader arrested.²⁴ Nolan, however, had already returned to the United States.

The following year, disregarding warnings not to enter Texas, Nolan and a party of men again entered the province. In March of 1801 they were surrounded north of present Waco by a force of 150 Spanish soldiers. In the ensuing struggle Nolan was killed and the remainder of his party captured.²⁵ As a result of this affair, Spanish suspicions about the designs of the United States grew.

Another factor contributing to the mounting Spanish distrust of the Anglo-Americans was the purchase of Louisiana in 1803 — an incident that almost led to war between the two nations three years later. The transfer of control of this province to the United States, effected December 15, 1803²⁶ immediately raised two problems: what should be done about the large number of Louisianans who wished to migrate to Texas, and exactly where was the boundary between the two provinces?

Governor Juan Bautista de Elguézabal²⁷ of Texas, who had succeeded Munoz, desired to populate the province under his command, and freely granted licenses to immigrants. But the new commandant-general Nemesio Salcedo Y Salcedo,²⁸ did not agree. On January 9, 1804, he wrote the governor of Texas that no individual proceeding from Louisiana was to be allowed to settle in the Eastern Interior Provinces. They could move to New Spain, but only to the interior.²⁹ Two months later, however, Salcedo's order was countermanded by a royal decree approving the resettlement of Louisianans in the Interior Provinces. The only proviso was that they could not live at Nacogdoches because they might be tempted to smuggle.³⁰ After the arrival of the king's order, the influx of settlers to Texas from the neighboring territory doubled and redoubled, ending only with the Neutral Ground settlement of 1806.³¹

A greater problem for the Spaniards than the peaceful settlers was the deserters from the United States Army and the fugitive slaves who made their way to Texas and asked for asylum.³² The Spaniards feared that the deserters were spies, and the owners of the runaway slaves protested loudly. The commandant-general finally issued an order that any deserter about whom there was the slightest suspicion was to be returned immediately to the American authorities; the rest were to be removed as far west as San Antonio, as were all slaves.[33]

The other problem raised by the Louisiana Purchase — the exact boundary — was an old one. The American government had merely inherited a dispute that dated back to the years preceding 1763, when Spain had acquired Louisiana from France and rendered the question academic. Many Americans believed that the Louisiana Purchase included Texas, and began noisily asserting a claim to it.[34] The Spaniards not only resisted such demands, but asserted a counterclaim. In Madrid the Council of State in March 1804 delineated the boundary as Spain felt it to be: from the Gulf of Mexico up the Arroyo Hondo to the vicinity of Natchitoches, and up the Red River. The boundary in the north, the Council asserted, was the Missouri River.[35]

Local Spanish officials disagreed about the exact boundary. The Marquis de Casa-Calvo, Spanish consul in New Orleans, believed the Sabine was the dividing line. Governor Elguézabal thought the line should be drawn according to the boundary set in the treaty of 1800 which returned Louisiana to France. Commandant-General Salcedo said nothing at all; instead, he sent a detachment of troops to occupy a position at Bayupier (Bayou Pierre) near the abandoned Spanish presidio of Los Adaes. He further ordered that no Americans whatsoever be allowed to approach the area to survey a boundary until the royal government designated a commission for that purpose.[36]

Gradually Salcedo began shifting his troops in the Eastern Interior Provinces in order to be able to cope quickly with any emergency along the Texas-Louisiana boundary. By September of 1805 the number of soldiers in Texas had been increased from two hundred to five hundred and fifty. Governor Antonio Cordera y Bustamante,[37] new chief executive in the province, still was dissatisfied; he asked for an additional seven hundred men.[38] The commandant-general did the best he could under the circumstances, and by December 31 of that year there were seven hundred troops in Texas, 141 of them at Nacogdoches and its vicinity.[39]

Early in 1806 the boundary dispute began to boil in earnest. The mayor of Natchitoches, the American outpost nearest Texas, wrote the commandant at Nacogdoches, Captain Sebastian Rodríguez, asking an assurance "that there will be no more incursions or acts of violence committed by subjects of Spain on this side of the Sabine River, which is considered included in the territory of the United States." Furthermore, he requested that all Spanish troops east of the Sabine be removed.[40] Rodriguez replied that the Spaniards occupied their "own territory," and that patrols would continue to be sent as far east as the Arroyo Hondo until he received further orders from the commandant-general.[41] Rodríguez at first seemed ready to back his bold words with action. On February 2 word reached Nacogdoches that a large party of American private citizens intended to occupy the area in dispute. The captain issued a proclamation to Spaniards in East Texas calling upon them to fight:

> The time has arrived in which you should show that you are vassals of His Catholic Majesty. I want you to know that the United States, full of ambition and greed, intends to usurp from our sovereign . . . part of this province. . . . It has been intimated to me by the commandant of the American troops that if we do not evacuate the terrain [between the Arroyo Hondo and the Sabine] . . . they will take that unjust pretext to declare war on us. I have given orders to our troops not to abandon their posts except at the price of their lives. . . . And I believe that you, on your part, should do as much in defense of the country in which you have your families, your property, and your subsistence, those whose station permits it taking arms. In this way you will show your fidelity and patriotism.[42]

Just three days after this pronouncement, the Spanish troops east of the Sabine had a chance to demonstrate their bravery. Approximately 150 American private citizens, without official sanction, approached the Spanish outposts in the disputed territory, and the Spaniards withdrew without a fight.[43] Captain Rodríguez decided that war was imminent, that the Spaniards could not win, and that it would be bad for his career to command a losing engagement. He asked to be replaced, declaring that the situation was "critical" and that his troops and their horses were "exhausted."[44]

The commandant-general saw the explosive possibilities of the controversy with the United States and the need of a seasoned officer in the area. He sent Lieutenant Colonel Símon de Herrera, Governor of Nuevo Santander, to East Texas to take command of the military forces along the border. Herrera did not arrive at Nacogdoches until June,[45] by which time war seemed inevitable. He found that the American force at Natchitoches was estimated at 12,000 to 15,000 men. According to the rumors circulating, this force was going to overrun the disputed teritory and also take North Texas, then force this settlement on Spain by presenting an accomplished fact.[46] Hastily the Spaniards moved the militias of Nuevo Santander and Nuevo Leon, as well as regular troops from other areas, to East Texas. By June 1 a record high of 1,368 Spanish fighting men were gathered in Texas, of whom 883 were at Nacogdoches and its vicinity.[47]

High Spanish officials moved cautiously. From the king came orders to proceed carefully, but not to concede any of the disputed territory. Both the viceroy and the commandant-general echoed this feeling. Salcedo wrote Herrera: "do not begin the action or attack the Americans without an absolute certainty of evicting them. . . ."[48]

At the very instant that it seemed war would begin, Herrera and General James Wilkinson, the American commander in Louisiana, reached a dramatic settlement. Wilkinson proposed a compromise, Herrera agreed, and on November 4 they signed an accord providing that Spanish troops would withdraw west of the Sabine, American troops would withdraw east of the Arroyo Hondo, and a final settlement would be left to negotiation between the two governments.[49] Later, Herrera received the thanks and praise of both the viceroy and the commandant-general for the compromise — an act that amounted to disobedience of orders.[50]

Following this settlement, tensions gradually relaxed in East Texas, and the number of Spanish soldiers in the area was reduced. Not all points of contention between the United States and Spain were solved by the Wilkinson-Herrera agreement, however. Fugitive slaves continued to make their way to Texas, and their owners continued to demand their return. Deserters from the United States Army continued to reach Nacogdoches and ask for Spanish citizenship. And forbidden books, spreading what Commandant-General Salcedo termed the "depraved . . . maxims of liberty and disunion," continued to be introduced into the New World Spanish colonies.[51]

To offset the possibility of further American expansion, Spanish officials in the Eastern Interior Provinces made attempts between 1806 and 1808 to increase the population of Texas by establishing new towns and by sending immigrants from Mexico. Between San Antonio and Nacogdoches at the Trinity River, the settlement of Trinidad de Salcedo was founded during the last week in December of 1805. Five families from San Antonio were joined there by a detachment of soldiers and twenty-three former Louisianans. Gradually the little village grew, until by March of 1809 it had a population of ninety-two.[52] Also established was the smaller settlement of San Marco de Neve at the spot where the road between San Antonio and San Juan Bautista (on the Rio Grande) crossed the San Marcos River. Financed personally by Governor Cordero, this village drew its settlers from Mexico. The founding date was January 6, 1808. Four months later the population numbered sixty-one, including a detachment of soldiers sent to guard the civilians from the Indian raiders.[53]

Two final incidents disturbed the slumber of Spanish officials in the Eastern Interior Provinces during the last years before the storm of revolution broke in New Spain: the appearance of Lieutenant Zebulon Pike, and the American Embargo Act. Most Spanish officials, including Commandant-General Salcedo, believed that the Pike Expedition was part of a continuing American plot to acquire territory that belonged to Spain. Salcedo felt that Pike's specific purpose was to subvert the loyalty of the Plains Indians. Therefore, as a counter measure, the commandant-general in 1808 ordered an expedition to march from San Antonio to Santa Fe, giving medals and flags to the various chiefs and exhorting them to retain their allegiance to Spain. Pike's expedition had consisted of himself, a doctor, and seventeen soldiers; the Spanish expedition was made up of two hundred soldiers. Furthermore, Salcedo took steps to stop the illegal immigration of American settlers to Texas, giving specific orders to the governor of the province to arrest such intruders. Governor Cordero agreed with his superior; in October of 1808 he wrote: "We must assume . . . that the inundation of vagrants, who have been introducing themselves into the area [of North Texas] is nothing more than a plot by that government [the United States] to take the land, and . . . realize, in succession, their ideas of conquest."[54]

The second cause of contention during the last years before revolution developed in the Interior Provinces, and in all of the Spanish New World colonies, was the American Embargo Act. Because of the disturbances in Europe, the Spaniards had been purchasing in the United States the goods which they annually distributed to the Indians as presents. Spanish officials saw the embargo as an insidious American ploy to win away the allegiance of the Indian tribes in Texas and perhaps to cause uprisings and raids by disgruntled natives in the Interior Provinces.[55]

Besides the problems with the United States, the representatives of the king in the Interior Provinces were further disturbed by events in Europe. In 1808 Spain again did a turnabout in the involved Napoleonic Wars, declaring a war on France and allying itself with England following the forced abdication of Ferdinand VII. Salcedo and his fellow officers feared that representatives of the new French regime in Spain might attempt to take control of the colonies. The commandant-general ordered a careful inventory of all weapons held by the inhabitants of Texas, and he filled the officer ranks in the army to full complement.[56] And he ordered that any Spaniard or Frenchman who presented himself in the Interior Provinces claiming to be a representative of the French regime in Spain was to be arrested immediately; he declared that such individuals were "traitors" to the "beloved king" and religion of Spain.[57]

In San Antonio two councils were held in connection with the new crisis. Convened by Brigadier Bernardo Bonavía, Salcedo's second-in-command, these councils were attended by Cordero, Herrera, and the new governor of Texas, Manuel de Salcedo. These gatherings were the last displays of pomp and ceremony in the province while Spain ruled it. Bonavía was met outside San Antonio by a military reception. Three days later, April 17, 1809, the first council convened to discuss military affairs in the Eastern Interior Provinces, and specifically the needs of Texas. The usual recommendations followed: more troops were needed, Nacogdoches should be garrisoned more strongly, and immigrants should be brought to populate the area between the Sabine River and San Antonio.[60]

Commandant-General Salcedo proved cold to these proposals, however. He was distrustful of foreigners and therefore was against the colonization scheme. Furthermore, he believed that in defending Texas all available strength should be concentrated at San Antonio, not at Nacogdoches. He had previously ordered that the road between San Antonio and Nacogdoches deliberately be left in a state of disrepair in order to slow an invading army.[61]

The second council was held in July of 1809 and discussed ways to improve the economy in Texas. The major recommendation of this meeting was that La Bahía be declared a port in order to facilitate the importation and exportation of goods.[62] But again the commandant-general turned a deaf ear. He declared that it was "very remote" that La Bahia could be opened successfully as a port.[63]

The two councils at San Antonio represented the last chance for the Spaniards to rejuvenate the economy of Texas and to institute reforms that would benefit the entire Eastern Interior Provinces. However, the same fear and distrust of change that máde these officials resist the French ideas of equality and the American idea of frontier democracy also caused them to resist altering the status quo in the provinces under their command. Thus as the year 1810 dawned the soil was prepared for revolution, which in turn would further weaken and depopulate the provinces and lay them open to filibusters.

Notes

1. First created in 1776, the Interior Provinces were administered by a commandant-general whose headquarters was at Arizpe or Chihuahua City. Then in 1787 the area was divided into the Eastern and Western Interior Provinces with separate commanders. Three years later the two commands were rejoined and placed under Brigadier Pedro de Nava. For further information about the founding of the Interior Provinces, see Alfred B. Thomas, **Teodoro de Croix and the Northern Frontier of New Spain, 1776-1783** (Norman, 1941), 16-20; and H. Bailey Carroll and J. Villasana Haggard (trans. and eds., **Three New Mexico Chronicles** (Albuquerque, 1942), 169-171.

2. Brigadier Pedro de Nava assumed command of the Interior Provinces on April 27, 1790. A combination of old age and poor health eventually forced him to request retirement from the royal service, a request that was granted. His replacement arrived on November 4, 1802, and Nava returned to Spain to enjoy his remaining years in peace and comfort. See El Conde de Revilla Gigedo to the governor of Texas, September 17, 1790, Mexico City, Béxar Archives (Archives, The University of Texas, Austin); Nava to Juan Bautista de Elguézabal, September 4, 1802, Chihuahua, Béxar Archives; and Nemesio Salcedo to the Governor of Texas, November 4, 1802, San Bartolomé, Béxar Archives. The Béxar Archives are hereinafter cited as BA.

3. Lieutenant-Colonel Manuel Muñoz became governor of Texas on August 14, 1790, and served in this capacity until his death on July 27, 1799. See Muñoz to Antonio Gil Ybarbo, August 16, 1790, San Antonio, BA; Francesco Xavier de Uranga to Elguézabal, August 3, 1799, La Bahía, BA.

4. Nava to the Governor of Texas, secret, November 30, 1793, Chihuahua, BA.

5. Nava to Muñoz, March 27, 1794, Chihuahua, BA.

6. Nava to Muñoz, very secret, January 6, 1795, Chihuahua, BA; Muñoz to Nava, No. 266, February 28, 1795, San Antonio, BA.

7. Juan Cortes to Muñoz, January 29, 1796, La Bahía, BA, contains notice of the peace treaty.

8. Nava to the Governor of Texas, November 21, 1794, Chihuahua, BA.

9. Nava to Muñoz, October 7, 1795, Chihuahua, BA.

10. Nava to Muñoz, October 12, 1796, Chihuahua, BA.

11. Muñoz to Nava, No. 498, February 27, 1797, San Antonio, BA, notes receipt of the declaration of war.
12. Muñoz to Nava, No. 537, August 6, 1797, San Antonio, BA.
13. Muñoz to Nava, No. 265, February 19, 1795, San Antonio, BA.
14. Nava to Muñoz, very secret, July 30, 1795, Chihuahua, BA.
15. Muñoz to Nava, No. 473, December 5, 1796, San Antonio, BA.
16. Nava to Muñoz, secret, August 28, 1798, Chihuahua, BA.
17. Nava to Muñoz, secret, October 13, 1798, Chihuahua, BA.
18. Ellis P. Bean, "Memoirs of Ellis P. Bean," quoted in Henderson Yoakum, History of Texas (2 vols.; Austin, 1935), I, 403-452; Rupert N. Richardson, Texas: The Lone Star State (Englewood Cliffs, New Jersey, 1943), 50.
19. Baron de Carondolet to Muñoz, September 9, 1794, New Orleans, BA; Muñoz to Carondolet, January 18, 1795, San Antonio, BA.
20. Nava to Philip Nolan, October 31, 1797, Chihuahua, BA.
21. Nava to Muñoz, March 20, 1798, March 20, 1798, Chihuahua, BA.
22. Nava to Muñoz, April 30, 1799, Chihuahua, BA.
23. Muñoz to Nava, No. 660, June 12, 1799, San Antonio, BA.
24. Ibid., notes this order.
25. Bean, "Memoirs," quoted in Yoakum, History of Texas, I, 403-452; Bennett Lay, The Lives of Ellis P. Bean (Austin, 1960), 13-25. One member of the Nolan party, Steven Richard, was in San Antonio in 1809 serving a ten-year sentence in the militia of Nuevo Leon and Nuevo Santander for his participation in the expedition; see Nemesio Salcedo to Manuel de Salcedo, March 23, 1809, Chihuahua, BA.
26. Francisco de Ugarte to Elguezabal, February 4, 1804, Nacogdoches, BA, contains the news of the change of control at New Orleans. However, the last Spanish governor-general of Louisiana, the Marquis de Casa-Calvo, wrote Elguézabal, that the American commissioners arrived on December 20. See Casa-Calvo to Elguézabal, March 5, 1804, New Orleans, BA.
27. Lieutenant Colonel Juan Bautista de Elguézabal became governor of Texas on July 27, 1799. He served until his September 10, 1805, when he was relieved because of ill health. He died in San Antonio on October 5 of that same year. See Urango to Elguézabal, August 3, 1799, La Bahía, BA; Nava to the Ayuntamiento of San Fernando of the Province of Texas, August 17, 1799, Chihuahua, BA; Cordero, Notarized Statement, December 23, 1805, San Antonio, BA. Elguezabal was replaced as governor by Antonio Cordero y Bustamente. One of Elguézabal's sons, Juan José, also served as governor of Texas in 1834-1835, when Texas and Coahuila were joined as one state; see Walter P. Webb (ed.), The Handbook of Texas (3 vols.; Austin, 1952), I, 554.
28. Upon the retirement of Pedro de Nava, Brigadier Nemesio

Salcedo y Salcedo became commandant-general, serving from November 4, 1802, until 1813. A stern man, he stubbornly clung to the old order and blocked progress and change whenever he could. See Salcedo to the Governor of Texas, November 4. 1802, San Bartolomé, BA; Elliott Coues (ed.), The Expeditions of Zebulon Pike (3 vols.; New York, 1895), II, 656; Webb (ed.), Handbook of Texas, I, 71.

29. Elguézabal to Salcedo, February 15, 1804, San Antonio, BA, notes the commandant-general's order of January 9.

30. Salcedo to Elguézabal, March 27, 1804, notes this royal order.

31. Mattie Austin Hatcher, The Opening of Texas to Foreign Settlement, 1801-1821 (Austin, 1927), 60-101.

32. Ugarte to Elguézabal, November 26, 1803, Nacogdoches, BA; Elguézabal to Salcedo, No. 311, November 7, 1804, San Antonio, BA.

33. Cordero to the Commandant at Nacogdoches, secret, September 30, 1805, San Antonio, BA, notes this instruction.

34. For the justice of the American claim to the Rio Grande as the boundary of the Louisiana Purchase, see Richard Stenberg, "The Western Boundary of Louisiana, 1762-1803," The Southwestern Historical Quarterly, XXXV (October 1931), 95-108.

35. Council of State, Decree, March 17, 1804, Madrid, Spain, BA. This decree did not give a north-south boundary between the Missouri and Red rivers.

36. Casa-Calvo to Elguézabal, June 19, 1804, New Orleans, BA; Elguézabal to Ugarte, March 4, 1804, San Antonio, BA; Salcedo to Elguézabal, May 3, 1804, Chihuahua, BA; Sebastian Rodríguez to Cordero, November 4, 1805, Nacogdoches, Nacogdoches Archives (Archives, Texas State Library, Austin). President Jefferson's attempts to send scientific expeditions up the Red River in 1804-1806 were also suspect by the commandant-general; he feared these expeditions were merely disguised attempts to survey a boundary prejudicial to Spanish interests. Therefore he ordered the Dunbar and the Freeman and Sparks expeditions turned back. See Salcedo to Cordero, secreta, October 8, 1805, Chihuahua, BA; Coues (ed.), The Expeditions of Zebulon Pike, II, 70. Likewise suspect in the eyes of Salcedo were the foreigners in Nacogdoches in 1804. He ordered all of them listed and carefully accounted for. The census for Nacogdoches in 1804 showed twenty Americans, eleven Irish, two Englishmen, eighteen French, one Scotsman, and fourteen Louisiana-born French; Ugarte, "Padron que manifiesta los Extrangeros que tiene este Pueblo, y toda su jurisdicion . . . ," January 1, 1804, Nacogdoches, BA.

37. Colonel Manuel Antonio Cordero y Bustamente arrived in San Antonio on September 8, 1805, and two days later assumed the governorship of the province. In addition, he was governor of Coahuila during this same period. An enlightened official, he hoped to admit to the province large numbers of bonafide settlers, both from Europe and the United States. He was relieved as governor of Texas on November 7, 1808, but stayed in the province until July 27, 1809. See Cordero,

Notarized Statement, December 23, 1805, San Antonio, BA; Cordero to Bernardo Bonavía, July 21, 1809, San Antonio, BA; Nettie Lee Benson, "Texas Failure to Send a Deputy to the Spanish Cortes, 1810-1812," **The Southwestern Historical Quarterly**, LXIV (July 1960), note on 21-22; Cordero to Bonavía, July 26, 1809, San Antonio, BA, contains the notice that Cordero was leaving Texas the following day.

38. Cordero to Nemesio Salcedo, No. 19, September 15, 1805, San Antonio, BA.

39. Cordero, "Provincia de los Texas. Fuerza de las Tropas que la guarnacion y su Distribucion actual . . . ," December 31, 1805, San Antonio, BA.

40. Mayor Porter to Rodríguez, translated into Spanish and quoted in Rodríguez to Salcedo, No. 12, January 30, 1806, Nacogdoches, BA.

41. Ibid.

42. Rodríguez, "Manifesto que hace el Capitan de Caballeria, Commandante del Puesto de Nacogdoches . . . a todos los havitantes de dicho Puesto y su Jurisdiccion, el 2 de Febrero de 1806 . . .,"February 2, 1806, Nacogdoches, BA.

43. José María González to Rodríguez, February 5, 1806, Arroyo de los Adaes, BA; Salcedo to Cordero, February 24, 1806, Chihuahua, BA.

44. Rodríguez to Cordero, No. 29, February 13, 1806, Nacogdoches, BA; Rodríguez to Cordero, No. 27, February 13, 1806, Nacogdoches, BA. This officer subsequently was brought to trial for his conduct during this period. A week later he was allowed to retire. See Salcedo to Cordero, March 25, 1806. Chihuahua, BA; Cordero to Salcedo, No. 636, September 28, 1807, San Antonio, BA.

45. Salcedo to Cordero, June 17, 1806, Chihuahua, BA; Viana to Cordero, June 6, 1806, Nacogdoches, BA.

46. Salcedo to Cordero, secret, April 19, 1806, Chihuahua, BA.

47. Miguel Serrano, "Estado que manifiesta la fuerza total y Desinos de las tropas que existen en esta Provincia," June 26, 1806, San Antonio, BA.

48. Salcedo to Cordero, secreta, October 24, 1806, Hazienda de los Ornos, BA; the king's order was contained in Salcedo to Cordero, very secret, March 17, 1807, Chihuahua, BA.

49. For Wilkinson's letter and Herrera's reply, see Ernest Wallace and David Vigness (eds.), **Documents in Texas History, 1528-1846** (Lubbock, Texas, 1960), I, 37-38.

50. Reported by Pike in Coues (ed.), **The Expeditions of Zebulon Pike**, II, 702-703.

51. Pedro Lopez Pieta to Manuel Salcedo, No. 3, November 22, 1808, Trinidad de Salcedo, BA, reported twenty-seven fugitive slaves at that settlement; Nemesio Salcedo to Cordero, December 9, 1806, San Antonio, BA, noted the presence of twenty American deserters in the capital city of Texas. Both types of unwanted immigrants subsequently were prohibited from entering the province; see Nemesio Salcedo to Cordero, December 2, 1808, Chihuahua, BA, and Nemesio Salcedo to Bonavía, July 9, 1809, Chihuahua, BA. About the forbidden books, see

Nemesio Salcedo to Cordero, secret, December 3, 1808, Chihuahua, BA.

52. Hatcher, **The Opening of Texas**, 102-103; Antonio Saens, "Padron General de toda la Jurisdicion de la Villa de Trinidad," March 22, 1809, Trinidad de Salcedo, BA.

53. Cordero to Felipe Roque de la Portilla, December 16, 1807, San Antonio, BA; Webb (ed.), **Handbook of Texas**, II, 558.

54. Francisco Amangual, "Diario de las Novedades y Operaciones occurridas en la Expedicion que se hace desde esta Provincia de Texas a la del Nuevo Mexico, de orden superior, siendo Primar Comandante el Capitan Don Francisco Amangual . . . ," March 30-December 23, 1808, San Antonio, BA; Cordero to Nemesio Salcedo, No. 3, very secret, October 15, 1808, San Antonio, BA. For an example of such illegal entry, see Manuel de Salcedo, "Texas. Causa seguida a los reos extrangeros Enrique Kuerke, Jose Magui, Juan Macfarzon y Jose Brenton . . . ," October 29, 1808-December 30, 1809, San Antonio, BA.

55. Cordero to Marzelo Soto, Very Secret, March 15, 1808, San Antonio, BA.

56. Cordero, "Pie de Lista, que manifiesta, los Yndibiduos que tiene las villa de San Fernando de Austria, capazes de podre tomar las Armas, con expresion, de los que estan armados, y montados . . . ," October 25, 1808, San Antonio, BA.

57. Nemesio Salcedo to Bonavía, June 22, 1808, Chihuahua, BA.

58. Because of the critical situation in Texas, the distance to Chihuahua City, and the slowness of communication, Salcedo in November of 1808 named Cordero Second Commandant-General. Cordero was relieved of this post in April of 1809 by Brigadier Bernardo Bonavía y Zapata. Like Cordero, Bonavía was liberal and enlightened, but he accomplished little in the way of reform in Texas during his short stay. See Nemesio Salcedo to Cordero, July 21, 1809, San Antonio, BA; Bonavía, Decree, April 19, 1809, San Antonio, BA.

59. Manuel María de Salcedo, the nephew of the commandant-general, assumed the governorship of Texas on November 7, 1808. He served during the revolutionary period that followed, and was executed by the filibusterer Bernardo Gutiérrez de Lara on April 3, 1813. See Cordero, Decree, November 7, 1808. San Antonio, BA; Harry McCorry Henderson, "The Magee Gutierrez Expedition," **The Southwestern Quarterly**, LV (July 1951), 46-52; Julia Kathryn Garrett, **Green Flag Over Texas** (New York, 1939), 17.

60. Bonavía, Cordero, Manuel de Salcedo, Herrera, and Mariano Varela, **Auto**, April 19, 1809, San Antonio, BA (Part of this document is missing); Garrett, **Green Flag Over Texas**, 21-22.

61. Manuel de Salcedo to Cordero, March 23, 1809, San Antonio, BA, communicates this information. See also Garrett, **Green Flag Over Texas**, 23.

62. Bonavía to Nemesio Salcedo, No. 55, July 26, 1809, San Antonio, BA.

63. Nemesio Salcedo to Bonavía, September 7, 1809, Chihuahua, BA.

2

La Salle
and the Historians

by
Ert J. Gum

Ert J. Gum is Professor of European History at the University of Nebraska at Omaha and the author of a study of Eugene Beauharnais.

2

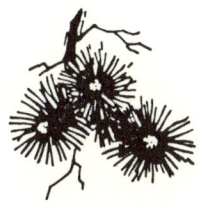

W. E. Dunn, in 1916, wrote that the story of the Texas expedition of Rene Robert Cavalier, Sieur de La Salle, an individual perhaps as well known as any other among the French explorers of North America, had been told in enough places that it needed no repetition, and apologized for another article on the subject.[1] It well may be that the story of La Salle in Texas needs no further investigation, at least as far as the skeletal outline is concerned, but a brief survey of some of the printed material published between 1856 and 1967 reveals that on several points, including some dates, there is little, if any, agreement among historians concerning the La Salle Texas expedition.

The first of the items about which writers disagree is the motive behind La Salle's attempt to establish himself in the southwest, which, for the purposes of this brief paper, will be understood to include present day Alabama and Louisiana. The second item on which there is no consensus is the intended location of the proposed colony — both La Salle's intended location and the location the government desired. Thirdly, the authors here surveyed are in general disagreement as to where La Salle went on two exploring trips. Finally, there is a difference of opinion concerning where he was killed; some recent writers of both monographs and textbooks give an erroneous impression as to the manner in which he met death, while a few have the wrong date for the killing.

Other than the authors of textbooks, those here reviewed have utilized the same sources. From the French side the sources have been primarily the Cavalier family papers, the French Marine (naval) archives, and the **Memorial Historique** of Henri Joutel, a member of the expedition to Texas; and from the Spanish side the archives of the Council of the Indies.

Real French interest in the southwest seems to have been sparked by the explorations of Marquette and Joliet in 1673. That interest soon changed into a desire to seize the Mississippi Valley, but for nine years the French in North America took no action to make the desire a reality. Then, in 1682, La Salle journeyed to the Gulf of Mexico and took possession of the territory in the name of His Most Catholic Majesty, Louis XIV. On these bare facts the historians here reviewed are all in agreement, and few current historians will find fault with them. They also all agree on the French "Grand Design" for North America once the government became interested in the southwest.

Troubles in Europe kept early governmental interest in abeyance, if it existed at all, and not until 1683 did the government actively become involved in the Mississippi Valley. The historians here examined are in agreement that government involvement stemmed from a memorial made by La Salle in late December, 1683, following his return to France in October of that year.[2] In his memorial La Salle proposed to establish a settlement on the Gulf of Mexico at the mouth of the Mississippi. Here the agreement of the historians surveyed comes to an abrupt end, with most in disagreement concerning La Salle's designs. Justin

Winsor, in his book, **Cartier to Frontenac,** suggest that in addition to other motives La Salle perhaps was motivated by personal greed, for La Barre, the then governor of Canada, had impoverished him through the seizure of his lands, goods, and frontier establishments.[3] Winsor also holds that early proposals indicate La Salle's interest was in commerce only.[4] However, in later proposals he added the element of conquest in that he proposed to attack New Biscay in the viceroyalty of New Spain and to seize the silver mines in that region.[5] The question, "Why did La Salle not mention his plans for conquest in his first proposal?" immediately rises. Winsor makes no attempt to answer the question, but Francis Parkman in his **La Salle and the Discovery of the Great West** suggests that La Salle was forced to introduce conquest because of his failure to interest the government in a commercial venture. Parkmen further holds that La Salle deliberately falsified the geographical relationship of the Red River and New Biscay, which he reported were only fifty leagues apart.[6] He agrees, however, that La Salle may have contemplated conquest at a later date.[7]

Bernard de Voto, in his **The Course of Empire,** accepts Parkman's view on this point as well as the idea that conquest was added to interest the Sun King,[8] as does E. T. Miller in an article entitled "The Connection of Penalosa with the La Salle Expedition" published in the **Texas Historical Association Quarterly** in October, 1901.[9]

Carlos E. Castaneda, however, in his **The Finding of Texas 1519-1693,** makes little mention of commerce. He holds that the proposal made by La Salle was primarily a military one and hints that he proposed to be a continuing irritant to the Spanish.[10]

It will be recalled that I earlier made the statement that French governmental interest in the Mississippi stemmed from La Salle's proposals beginning in 1683. It should be noted that an earlier proposal for the conquest of New Spain made by Dom Diego Penalosa, a former governor of New Spain, had elicited no response from the French government. This might cast some doubt on Parkman's notion that La Salle introduced conquest to interest Louis XIV if it were not for the fact that war between Spain and France erupted in 1683. Penalosa's proposals closely resembled La Salle's, and our historians can no more agree on Penalosa and his relationship to the Frenchman and his Texas venture than on the motive question.

Parkman give Penalosa a footnote and suggests he may have affected La Salle's proposals,[11] but evidently feels there was no intimate connection between them. Others, however, give more attention to the problem. Winsor notes there was a "remarkable resemblance" between La Salle's and Penalosa's proposals,[12] while Castaneda flatly asserts that in February, 1684, an attempt was made (by whom he does not say) to join the proposals of the two men.[13] Miller disclaims any tangible connection between the two,[14] while De Voto maintains La Salle was forced to accept Penalosa's proposals.[15] Though there is no agreement on this point, all who mention Penalosa's plans agree on his proposals, which were to raise a force of buccaneers at Santo Domingo, invade New Spain at Panuco late in 1685, and drive to Durango. La Salle, on his part, proposed to raise 15,000 Indian warriors, advance up the Red River, turn to the south to attack New Biscay, join Penalosa and cut northern New Spain off from Mexico City, and perhaps even attack Mexico City itself.[16]

All who handle this question agree that for whatever reason, La Salle obtained his commission and Penalosa faded from the picture. In obtaining his commission La Salle received four ships, men and equipment, and the governorship of all land between Lake Michigan and the Gulf of Mexico.[17] All agree that command was split at sea with La Salle in command of the route and soldiers, while Captain Beaujeu of the Royal Navy commanded the sailors; such a split in command soon caused friction between the explorer and the sailor.[18]

Part of the friction, according to Winsor, was due to La Salle's resentment of Beaujeu's better judgment, a factor not mentioned by any other. However, both Winsor and Parkman mention La Salle's suspicions of Beaujeu because his wife was a confidant of the Jesuits, whom La Salle felt were responsible for his misfortunes.[19] While none of the others mention it, Parkman insists Beaujeu did his best to get along with La Salle, but La Salle's vile temper made it impossible.[20]

The friction began at La Rochelle, where they outfitted, and continued throughout the voyage. On this facet of the story, Parkman and Winsor are more descriptive than the others. Both record that La Salle refused to take on water at Madeira for fear of the Spanish gaining knowledge of the expedition.[21] Parkman and Castaneda mention that Beaujeu refused to put in at Port de Paix and sailed on to Petit Goave, which resulted in one ship becoming separated from the others and being captured by the Spanish.[22] Of this incident Winsor merely reports the capture due to the ship being separated from the others by a storm.[23]

All agree that La Salle was ill at Santo Domingo. Winsor and Castaneda suggest that his illness accounts for many desertions to buccaneers anchored there.[24] They all agree that not until late November could La Salle move out, now short one ship, and that he moved from Beaujeu's ship to the next largest one. Parkman claims that the reason for the move was that Aigron, Captain of the ship to which La Salle moved, threatened to quit the expedition due to La Salle's foul temper.[25]

From this point the writers here surveyed shift their emphasis to the question of where the little fleet went after leaving Santo Domingo and why. Parkman, on this point, claims no person aboard La Salle's fleet knew the Gulf of Mexico, even though he had recruited some fifty pirates while at Petit Goave. He insists La Salle and Beaujeu had been misled by reports of the strength of the currents in the Gulf of Mexico and as a result sailed too far to the west.[26] Both Parkman and Winsor make the claim that when they sighted land on December 28, 1684, La Salle and Beaujeu thought they had reached the northwest Florida coast and were in Appalachee Bay.[27] Winsor reports they were probably at Atchafalaya Bay, and Parkman ventures no guess.[28]

A dense fog settled on December 30 and lay on the water until well after January 1, 1685, and when it lifted revealed that Beaujeu's ship was not in sight. Parkman reports that on January 1, La Salle went to explore the coastline with a pilot, and in the dense fog found only marshes.[29]

Castaneda dates this event as January 10, and reports La Salle asserted he was too far east to be even near the Mississippi. Further, he believes La Salle probably knew where he was but would not admit it, and deliberately went past the river.[30] While Parkman asserts La Salle went ashore with the pilot, Castaneda claims he did not and that he ignored the pilot's report that he thought a river was there. Both Parkman and Castaneda report the north latitudinal location as approximately 29°, the approximate latitude of the Louisiana coast. Parkman claims La Salle did not know the longitude of the river[31] which, until 1770 and the invention of the chronometer, could not be determined.

Winsor and Parkman report that on January 1, 1685, La Salle was probably at the mouth of the Sabine River, and that on January 6, while looking for Beaujeu and his ship, which had become separated in the dense fog of December 31 and January 1, he probably discovered Galveston Bay.[32] Thus, between these historians there is no agreement except that he was off the southern coast of North America and in the Gulf of Mexico. It is evident that they even disagree on dates, though Winsor and Parkman generally agree; Castaneda, however, seems a bit careless on this point. Winsor further does not accept the notion that La Salle deliberately overshot the Mississippi,[33] but De Voto holds that missing the Mississippi was a part of the concessions to the government made by La Salle to obtain his commission to establish a settlement.[34] Only one thing is certain — he did not sail into or enter in any way the Mississippi River. From the foregoing, one might ask "what was his real intention," and our historians have.

Winsor contends that the documents indicate La Salle intended to establish his settlement some sixty leagues up the Mississippi. Castaneda claims he intended to settle sixty leagues down the coast (west) from that river, though he reports that La Salle proposed to Louis XIV to settle at the mouth of the river. Miller maintains the settlement was to be up the river toward Fort St. Louis on the Illinois.[35]

At any rate, they all agree La Salle spent most of the month of January, partly with Beaujeu with whom he made contact accidentally, exploring the Texas Coast and looking for his "fatal river." They are in agreement that finally, near mid-February, 1685, he decided to put his followers ashore at Matagorda Bay under the claim that it was the Mississippi. Only Parkman stoutly defends the position that La Salle thought he was on the Mississippi[36] and admits that La Salle finally accepted the fact he was not on his river only after making a brief exploration upon going ashore.[37] Winsor reports that La Salle wrote the Marquis de Seignelay that he was on the west mouth of the Mississippi and believed the main channel to be twenty to thirty leagues east, but soon gave up the notion and decided to establish a permanent camp from which to search for the river.[38] If La Salle thought he was on the west mouth, why did he not take one of his two remaining ships (one had been lost going ashore) and search for it? Or why not simply return to Santo Domingo if De Voto is correct in his assertion that La Salle wanted to give up before landfall had been made?[39]

All agree on the location of the camp site as being on the Garcitas River — except Parkman, who contends it was on the La Vaca River, so named from the number of buffalo grazing its banks.[40] The establishment of a fort is handled rather cursorily by all, the story varying only in the amount of detail recorded. In this area Parkman gives the most information, while Castaneda and Winsor are equally terse. At this point all are in agreement except Henderson Yoakum,[41] that La Salle knew he was not on his river and planned to explore to find it, but could not leave his little band before October, 1685. They agree he left on October 30, but on nothing else. Winsor reports it was an aimless march, lasting six months, netting nothing,[42] though he does report La

Salle said he had found the Mississippi and left six men in a palisade on it. They were never heard of again. Neither Fr. Charlevoix in his **Journal of a Voyage to North America**, nor N. Maynard Crouse in his study of d'Iberville make mention of finding such an outpost. Winsor apparently believes that on this trip La Salle probably journeyed to the north and east. Parkman asserts La Salle went south to Matagorda Bay and then turned eastward. He then gives details of existence at La Salle's small fort and brings him back at the end of March, 1686, without having found the river.[43] He reports that La Salle claimed he had met Indians who knew the Spanish and told him it would be easy to cross the Rio Grande. Here the palisade story is told, also.[44] Castaneda reiterates the story of his having met Indians who knew the Spaniards, and asserts that to have done so La Salle would perforce have been in present west Texas or perhaps even in New Mexico. He believes the explorer probably reached the Rio Grande.[45]

Having had no success, in mid-April, 1686, La Salle left again. All agree that he traveled in an easterly direction, though they only guess at how far east he advanced. Parkman says La Salle probably reached the Sabine. How far north he went also is conjecture, the only evidence resting in the fact that he did meet the Cenis, or Tejas, Indians and obtained from them a few horses.[46] Castaneda claims the Trinity as the major river reached, and has La Salle perhaps fifty miles south of Nacogdoches.[47] Hampered by weather, illness, and a shortage of powder he returned to his fort in August only to learn of the loss of his one remaining ship.[48] After a bout with "illness" and hernia he determined to go to the Illinois country for succor, and left early in January.

Parkman has him leaving on his last trip on the morrow of 12th night, January 7, 1687,[49] while Castaneda has him departing on January 12, 1687.[50] All agree that he took a northeasterly route and that movement was slow due to heavy rains and swollen rivers. They give no details of this journey until the time of his murder, the date and place of which is in dispute. Winsor simply puts the time as mid-March;[51] Parkman and

Yoakum set the day as March 19, 1687,[52] while Castaneda places the date as March 20.[53] Winsor places the spot of the killing on the Trinity[54]; Parkman near the Trinity,[55] and Castaneda the Navasota.[56]

Textbook authors have done even worse by the story than those who have researched it. By no means have I surveyed all textbooks on American history, but I have taken a few samplings.

Oliver Perry Chitwood in his **History of Colonial America** has a brief paragraph on the Texas venture, but La Salle does not appear in the index of the second edition of this work.[57] Curtis P. Nettles in his **The Roots of American Life**, 2nd edition, simply states that La Salle, in 1684, lost his life while attempting to establish a settlement on the Mississippi and capture the southern fur trade, with the possiblity of an attack on New Spain thrown in.[58] Note that Nettles has La Salle killed before he reached the coast. Ray Allen Billington in his **Westward Expansion** only states that La Salle intended to settle on the Mississippi, missed it, and that his followers rebelled and killed him,[59] which is in error. Incidentally, De Voto's account of La Salle's murder is suspiciously like Billington's, and De Voto has his death occurring in 1689.[60]

Survey texts are worse yet. John D. Hicks, George Mowry, and Robert Burke in their **The Federal Union**, latest edition, give the Texas attempt a couple of lines and use Nettles' date, 1684, for the murder.[61] Harry Carman, Harold Syrett, and Bernard Wishy in their **A History of the American People**, Vol. I, 2nd ed., make no mention of the great Frenchman in their section on exploration and settlement or in the section on French and British rivalry in North America.[62] La Salle suffers the same fate at the hands of Ralph Harlow and Nelson Blake in their **The United States**, 3rd ed., revised.[63]

I believe enough areas of disagreement have been suggested to indicate that Dunn, when he apologized in 1916 for publishing another article on La Salle's Texas venture, was mistaken in thinking the facts were then well enough known. It is an area in which the definitive work has not yet been written, and perhaps it cannot be; but it certainly warrants further investigation.

Notes

1. William E. Dunn, "The Spanish Search for La Salle's Colony on the Bay of Espiritu Santo, 1685-1689," Southwestern Historical Quarterly, Vol. 19, No. 4, (1916), 323.
2. Justin Winsor, Cartier to Frontenac. (Boston & New York, 1894), 308, Hereinafter cited as Winsor, Cartier to Frontenac.
3. Ibid., 310.
4. Ibid., 297.
5. Ibid., 309.
6. Francis Parkman, La Salle and the Discovery of the Great West. (Boston, 1899), 345-349. Hereinafter cited as Parkman, La Salle.
7. Ibid.
8. Bernard De Voto, The Course of Empire. (Cambridge, Massachusetts, 1952), 137. Hereinafter cited as De Voto, Empire.
9. E. T. Miller, "The Connection of Penalosa with the La Salle Expedition," Texas Historical Association Quarterly, Vol. 5, No. 2, 1901, 97-109. Hereinafter cited as Miller, "Penalosa."
10. Carlos E. Castaneda, The Finding of Texas, 1519-1693, "Our Catholic Heritage in Texas" Series. (Austin, 1936), 282. Hereinafter cited as Castaneda, Finding Texas.
11. Parkman, La Salle, 350.
12. Winsor, Cartier to Frontenac, 309.
13. Castaneda, Finding Texas, 282-283.
14. Miller, "Penalosa," 97-109.
15. De Voto, Empire,137.
16. Castaneda, Finding Texas, 281; 282-283; Parkman, La Salle, 345-349.
17. Winsor, Cartier to Frontenac, 310.
18. Castaneda, Finding Texas, 285; Parkman, LaSalle, 358.
19. Parkman, La Salle, 354; Winsor, Cartier to Frontenac, 311.
20. Parkman, La Salle, 354.
21. Winsor, Cartier to Frontenac, 310, 312; Parkman, La Salle, 366-367.
22. Parkman, La Salle, 368, Castaneda, Finding Texas, 285.
23. Winsor, Cartier to Frontenac, 312.
24. Ibid.
25. Parkman, La Salle, 372.
26. Ibid., 373.
27. Parkman, La Salle, 373; Winsor, Cartier to Frontenac, 312.
28. Ibid; Ibid.
29. Parkman, La Salle, 373.
30. Castaneda, Finding Texas, 286.
31. Ibid., 286, 287.
32. Parkman, La Salle, 374.

33. Winsor, Cartier to Frontenac, 312-313.
34. De Voto, Empire, 137.
35. Castaneda, Finding Texas, 282, 287; Winsor, Cartier to Frontenac, 282, 309; Miller, "Penalosa," 99.
36. Parkman, La Salle, 367-377; 378-379.
37. Ibid., 388-389.
38. Winsor, Cartier to Frontenac, 316-317.
39. De Voto, Empire, 138.
40. Parkman, La Salle, 392.
41. Henderson Yoakum, History of Texas From its First Settlement in 1685 to its Annexation to the United States in 1846. (New York, 1856), 22. Hereinafter cited as Yoakum, Texas.
42. Winsor, Cartier to Frontenac, 318, 319, 320.
43. Parkman, La Salle, 396-402.
44. Ibid., 403.
45. Castaneda, Finding Texas, 292-293.
46. Parkman, La Salle, 405-406; 411-417.
47. Castaneda, Finding Texas, 294-295.
48. Ibid., 293.
49. Parkman, La Salle, 417.
50. Castaneda, Finding Texas, 296-297.
51. Winsor, Cartier to Frontenac, 321.
52. Parkman, La Salle, 426-429; Yoakum, Texas, 40.
53. Castaneda, Finding Texas, 296-297.
54. Winsor, Cartier to Frontenac, 321.
55. Parkman, La Salle, 426-429.
56. Castaneda, Finding Texas, 296297.
57. Oliver Perry Chitwood, A History of Colonial America. (2nd ed.; New York, 1948), 372.
58. Curtis P. Nettles, The Roots of American Life. (2nd ed.; New York, 1963), 368.
59. Ray Allen Billington, Westward Expansion: A History of the American Frontier. (3rd ed.; New York, 1967), 432-33.
60. De Voto, Empire, 138.
61. John D. Hicks, et. al., The Federal Union.(4th ed.; Boston, 1964), 136.
62. Harry J. Carman, et. al., A History of the American People, Vol. I. (2nd ed.; New York, 1960), 1-50; 71-75.
63. Ralph Volney Harlow, The United States: From Wilderness to World Power. (3rd ed., Rev. be Nelson Blake: New York, 1957), 1-17; 63-67.

3

McMahan's Chapel: Landmark in Texas*

by
Walter N. Vernon

*A version of this article appeared in Methodist History for October, 1970, and is used here with permission.

Walter N. Vernon was born in Oklahoma, raised in Texas, and has spent most of his life as an editor, journalist, and author in Nashville, Tennessee with the Methodist Church. He is Conference Historian for the North Texas Conference and Chairman, South Central Jurisdiction, of the Archives and History Commission.

3

An area in East Texas that was the passageway in 1812-20 of freebooters, filibusters, spies, soldiers, and settlers[1] became the location in 1833 of what seems to be the oldest Protestant Church with continuous history in Texas — McMahan's Chapel. There were Methodist churches or "societies" in Northeast Texas along Red River as early as 1815, established by the Rev. William Stevenson, but none begun there before 1833 seem to have survived.

The area in which McMahan's Chapel is located is Sabine County, adjoining Louisiana. While under Mexican rule there were restrictions against settlements within twenty leagues of the boundary of Texas, and this encouraged drifters and squatters, delaying permanent settlement. In 1812 Gaines Ferry was established across the Sabine River, making easier the route from Natchitoches, Louisiana to San Augustine and Nacogdoches, Texas. This route was variously called the King's Highway (it was authorized by the king of Spain in 1691, and established in that year by Domingo Terran de los Rios, first provincial governor of Texas),[2] the old Spanish Highway, the old San Antonio Road, and El Camino Real. It became the principal land route to Texas from about 1815 to 1850. As an example, Jared E. Groce migrated over this route in 1821-22 from Alabama to Texas with a caravan of more than fifty covered wagons, plus men on horseback herding horses, mules, oxen, cows, sheep, and hogs.[3]

In 1829 Lorenzo Manuel de Zavala received an empresario's contract to settle 500 families in the area east of the Sabine River including Nacogdoches and San Augustine. In 1834 he sold his contract to the Galveston Bay and Texas Land Company, and its agents conveyed many titles to early settlers.[4]

In 1831 Samuel Doak McMahan moved from his home near Doak's Crossing in Tennessee to Sabine County, locating near Polly Gotch Creek Valley, some ten or twelve miles northeast of San Augustine. His land title, dated October 11, 1835, is identified as a part of Zavala's Colony.[5]

Samuel Doak McMahan was born in Tennessee on November 5, 1789, according to family information and the U. S. Census.[6] His birthplace may have been Washington County, for (1) county records show that there were several McMahon or McMahan families in the county at that time, (2) Washington County was the home of a famous Presbyterian preacher in Washington County, the Rev. Samuel Doak for whom he may have been named, and (3) it is possible that his wife's family or relatives also came from that county.[7] Incidentally, present students of the family line are convinced the name was spelled McMahon, but the McMahan spelling has become so fixed in regard to McMahan's Chapel that it is used herein.

McMahan was in Smith County, Tennessee by 1803, when he was married to Phoebe Young. Smith County at that time was a strong Methodist center; among other more famous Methodists there was William Stevenson[8] whose son, James Porter, organized the society at McMahan's Chapel in 1833, as we shall see later.

McMahan may have been influenced by the Methodists, but so far as we know he did not join them until he was in Texas. There is evidence that McMahan moved to other parts of Tennessee before going to Texas, but we are not able to trace his itinerary, although there were other McMahans during these years in Marion, Lawrence, and Lincoln counties. Nor have we discovered the location of Doak's Crossing in Tennessee, from which, tradition says, he went to Texas.

When McMahan arrived at his new Texas home, it was still a part of the Mexican government, being in the San Augustine municipality. He built his home of logs on a site at the brow of a hill, and some remaining stones from the fireplace are still to be seen.[9] He is described as a seeker of religion while still in Tennessee by Homer S. Thrall, who also says that "while engaged in secret prayer on the bank of Aish Bayou in 1832 he was happily converted."[10]

Having come to this new religious experience, McMahan naturally wanted to conserve and extend it to others. For one thing, he had a large and growing family for whom he desired religious nurture. His children — and the years of their births — were Elizabeth Moor (1813), James B. (1814), Merlin Young (1816), Susan Young (1817), Alabama Tennessee (1820), Nancy Hardin (1823), Diana Lucina (1828), Margaret Tabitha (1831), and Louisa Holman (1834). He was concerned to find a preacher for his area of the country. He was undoubtedly aware that Methodist circuit riders were already active in northeastern Texas, southwestern Arkansas, and northwestern Louisiana, not far from his home.

Methodist preaching had been introduced into northeastern Texas along Red River in the winter of 1815. The Rev. William Stevenson had preached at Pecan Point in Red River County in that year, and in succeeding years he and others (including Henry Stephenson) extended the circuits on both sides of the river. Soon Stevenson, as the presiding elder in Arkansas, was investigating possibilities for evangelizing other parts of Texas. The chief obstacle to Methodist preaching in Texas was the Mexican prohibition of any but the Roman Catholic religion. Stevenson had a series of letters with Stephen F. Austin, the Texas colonizer, in which Austin wrote that "if a METHODIST, or any other PREACHER except a CATHOLIC, was to go through this colony preaching, I should be compelled to IMPRISON HIM."[11]

At about this time the Rev. Henry Stephenson, a close friend and colleague of William Stevenson, made a trip into Texas visiting some of the Methodists they had both nurtured earlier in northeastern Texas. Undoubtedly, Stevenson, as Henry's presiding elder, knew of this trip and may well have encouraged it in order to learn if Methodist preaching was possible. The Rev. J. P. Sneed wrote that about 1823 "Brother [William] Gates and a few others once and awhile united in the service of God. About one year after they had settled [in 1822] an old acquaintance (Henry Stephenson, a Methodist preacher) visited them and preached for them and a few other neighbors, not desiring to let it be known publicly."[12] Stephenson also preached at other places, as quietly as possible.

All of this preaching, however, evidently raised Austin's ire, for soon he wrote to his sister: "The Methodists have raised the cry against me . . . if they are kept out, or would remain quiet if here for a short time we shall succeed in getting a free toleration for all Religions, but a few fanatic and imprudent preachers at this time would ruin us . . . ."[13]

Austin was fearful that too much public preaching would have serious consequences on the effort to gain the larger goal of religious toleration: "I am of opinion that no evils will arise from family or neighborhood worship . . . provided it is not done in a way to make a noise about public preaching. So as not to start excited Methodist preachers, for I do say that in some instances they are too fanatic, too violent and too noisy . . . I do assure you that it will not do to have the Methodist excitement raised in this country."[14]

In 1825-26 Stevenson moved to Claiborne Parish, Louisiana, accompanied by the Rev. Henry Stephenson. William transferred his membership to the Mississippi

Conference (which then included Louisiana), and Henry joined it in 1830. Henry seems to have continued his visits to old Methodist friends in East Texas, sometimes preaching, we would assume. In 1831 James Porter Stevenson, William's son, joined the Mississippi Conference; in the fall of 1832 he was appointed to the Sabine Circuit in Louisiana, with Natchitoches as the headquarters. He soon heard of the desire of Texas Methodists to secure preachers, among these being Samuel Doak McMahan. Stevenson told a friend of the events that followed, and here is what the friend reported:

> "In May, 1833, casually meeting with some Texans in a store in the town of Natchitoches, they invited him [James Porter Stevenson] to preach in Texas. His response was 'I am afraid.' It was then a penal offense for any Protestant to preach the gospel in Texas. The Texans . . . Lowe and Milton . . . insisted . . . . Speaking in a firm, resolute voice he [Milton] said, 'You come; I'll stand at your back; you shan't be hurt.' Brother Stevenson consented. The programme fixed upon was a two days' meeting at John Smith's, in Sabine County, where Milam, the first county seat, now stands, with an appointment at Mr. Lowe's house on the preceding Friday. True to time, Bro. Stevenson . . . set out for Lowe's Ferry. Passing safely through the floods of the Sabine a half mile or more, he found the faithful ferryman in readiness to set him across and conduct him to his house, where a large congregation was in waiting to hear the word, in defiance of the laws of Mexico.
>
> "Mr. Milton was 'at his back' per promise, with whom he lodged on Friday night, and by whom he was piloted to Uncle Johnny Smith's. A very large congregation was in waiting . . . on Sabbath at 11 o'clock . . . .
>
> "Samuel D. McMahan, a citizen living a few miles in the interior, sent the preacher a verbal invitation to preach at his house on the following Monday. The congregation at Mr. McMahan's was large, some coming eight or ten miles. This, Bro. Stevenson thinks, was the first Methodist preaching ever done in this section of Texas . . . . Brother S. returned to Louisiana, the Texans having prevailed on him to hold a camp-meeting, embracing the 4th of July. The place selected was on the Polly-gotch [sic], in Sabine Parish,[15] where McMahan's Chapel now stands . . . The meeting was held at the appointed time and continued three days . . . . This meeting resulted in several conver-

sions. The people demanded another camp-meeting to be held in September following.

"This [September] meeting was on a larger scale. Bro. Stevenson was assisted by Bros. McKinney, Gordon, and Dawdy. On Sunday evening the people clamored for the organization of a church. What was to be done? The laws of Mexico positively forbade such organization, under heavy penalties. The knot difficult to untie may be cut. The pioneer preacher organized a church de facto in the wilderness but prudently styled it a society. Let who will make capital of this fact.

"The first church in the Red lands of Texas was composed of forty-eight members, nearly all of whom were genuine believers, truly regenerate persons. The rest professed to have a desire to flee the wrath to come. With a promise to visit them again in October, the preacher left the flock under the care of Bro. McMahan, whom he had appointed class leader. This promise was redeemed and a two-days meeting was held, in which Rev. Enoch N. Talley, of the Mississippi Conference, rendered efficient aid. Great and lasting good resulted from this meeting . . . ."

This account appeared in the **Texas Christian Advocate** of September 18, 1880 and was signed "H". The writer was almost certainly James W. Hill, a long-time resident of Hunt County, a prolific writer of articles and several books, and editor of **The North Texas Pulpit** (1880). The account says that he and James P. Stevenson worked together in a protracted meeting at Shady Grove, Hunt County, in 1880, and evidently Stevenson talked at length about his early ministry in Texas.

Charter members of the society/church formed at McMahan's home included Colonel and Mrs. Samuel Doak McMahan, three of their daughters and their husbands; Mr. and Mrs. J. T. P. Irvine, Mr. and Mrs. Acton Young, Mr. and Mrs. E. P. Chisholm; and the Colonel's son and his wife, Mr. and Mrs. James B. McMahan; Mr. and Mrs. Willis Murphy, Martha Murphy Drawhon and her husband, and Mr. and Mrs. W. A. Thompson.

Across the years there has been some difference of opinion regarding the dates and the founder of this society/church, due to a statement from the Rev. J. P. Sneed, quoted and accepted by the Rev. Macum Phelan in his **History of Early Methodism in Texas, 1817-1866**. Sneed wrote, "The society that Bro. James

Stevenson formed and never met was scattered. Henry Stephenson formed one [in 1834] and appointed Bro. McMahan leader. This society remains to this day [1873]."[16] Obviously no one wishes to detract any credit or honor from either of these two fine men. Each labored sacrificially for his Lord. It is clear that Henry Stephenson made numerous preaching tours into both Northeast and East Texas long before 1833. But the account above of James P. Stevenson's work at McMahan's states specifically that he first preached there soon after May, 1833, again over the Fourth of July, again in September, and again in October in company with Rev. Enoch N. Talley. All of this sounds like a fairly well established society, and gives ground for concluding that the 1833 society beginning under James P. Stevenson was a continuing one.[17] Yet each man contributed significantly to establishing Methodism in Texas.

Class leader McMahan was given the title of "colonel" because of his commanding one of the battalions in the fight with Piedras at Nacogdoches. He was licensed as a local preacher by the Rev. Robert Alexander in 1837. The three sons-in-law mentioned above all became traveling preachers.

After Texas independence was achieved, the members of the group at McMahan's set out to erect a house for their worship. Soon, under the leadership of the Rev. Littleton Fowler, they had completed a meeting house, thirty by forty feet, made of pine logs, hewed flat. C. A. West dates the building in 1836, Homer S. Thrall in 1838, and Macum Phelan in both 1838 and 1839! At that time it was named McMahan's Chapel; a contemporary called it a "rude log-chapel."[19] When Fowler died in 1846, he was buried under the pulpit of the Chapel, and as successive buildings have been erected, the grave has been retained under the pulpit. Fowler had made his home in the McMahan area before his death.

The church continued to grow and in 1872 a frame structure was built. A third building was dedicated in 1900; a story in the **Houston Post** for August 12, 1900 said that over a thousand people gathered for the dedication on July 28. The present brick structure was dedicated by Bishop A. Frank Smith on July 19, 1956, with the Rev. C. A. West presiding as chairman of the Texas Conference Historical Society.

Methodist historians have considered McMahan's Chapel the oldest Protestant congregation in Texas with continuous existence. This claim seems likely to be true. The nearest claim to challenge McMahan's Chapel is that of the Presbyterian Church in Clarksville. The best evidence about the beginnings of the Presbyterian Church seem to place it about December 1, 1833 or even early in 1834. This is the conclusion of a recent pastor, the Rev. Raymond Judd, Jr., after he had examined all the available evidence.

The Chapel has a special board of trustees consisting in part of the representatives of the Texas Conference and of the San Augustine District. The annual conference provides certain funds to help maintain the Chapel. It has about thirty members, but average attendance on Sunday mornings is often more than that. An adult church school class has about thirty members and an average attendance of twenty to twenty-five. The building is valued at about $50,000. Four churches in the area comprise the McMahan's Chapel Circuit.

In addition to regular services two Sundays each month, the church has an annual reunion/celebration on the second Thursday in July each year.

Notes

1. Dan Ferguson in Walter P. Webb (ed.), **The Handbook of Texas**, 523-4. Austin: Texas. (3 vols.; Austin, 1952-1977), II, 523-4.

2. Ibid., 309.

3. William Ransom Hogan: **The Texas Republic**. (Norman; 1946), 5-6.

4. Archie P. McDonald, "Westward I Go Free — Some Aspects of Early East Texas Settlement" in **East Texas Historical Journal**. (October, 1966), IV, 78.

5. An Abstract of the Original Titles of Record in the General Land Office [of Texas], 1838. Reprinted by Pemberton Press, Austin, 1964, 145-6.

6. Letter from Mrs. N. I. Hurst, Newton, Texas, dated January 3, 1969.

7. McMahan was married to Phoebe Young, daughter of Merlin Young, in Smith County, Tennessee on April 26, 1811 (according to

Mrs. Hurst). Smith County records also show the names of William and John Young, and in Washington County we find a few years earlier the names of William, John, and "Phebee" Young (county records in Tennessee State Archives and Library).

8. See Walter N. Vernon: **William Stevenson, Riding Preacher.** (Dallas, 1964),

9. C. A. West. **McMahan's Methodist Chapel.** Four page booklet, no date, no publisher.

10. Homer S. Thrall: **A Brief History of Methodism in Texas.** (Nashville, 1894), 24.

11. Written May 30, 1824. Printed in **Arkansas Gazette,** August 29, 1824, 3.

12. Macum Phelan: **A History of Early Methodism in Texas, 1817-1866.** (Nashville, 1924), 33.

13. To Mrs. James F. Perry, December 17, 1824 in **Annual Report of the American Historical Association for the Year 1919,** Vol. II, **The Austin Papers,** Part I, 991-2. Edited by Eugene C. Barker. (Washington, 1924).

14. Austin to Josiah H. Bell, February 24, 1829, in **Annual Report of the American Historical Association for the Year 1922,** Vol. II, **The Austin Papers,** (for 1828-1834), 173-74.

15. This should obviously be Sabine County; Sabine Parish was just across the Sabine River in Louisiana.

16. Phelan, **A History of Methodism in Texas,** 29.

17. As early as 1856, H. Yoakum in his **History of Texas** (New York, II, 221) stated that a Methodist church had been established in 1833 ten miles east of San Augustine, acknowledging it as one of, if not the first, churches "in the Texas wilderness."

18. C. A. West, **McMahan's Methodist Church,** 2; Homer S. Thrall, **A Brief History of Methodism in Texas,** 53; Macum Phelan, **A History of Methodism in Texas,** 30, 257. The Rev. Robert Alexander entered Texas as one of the three first official missionaries at Gaines Ferry on August 19, 1837. He has stated that a few days later he held a camp meeting for the McMahan society and that "on Sunday, during the service, rain fell gently for over an hour on the unsheltered audience, yet no one left." (Yoakum, **History of Texas,** II, 539). This would seem to place the date for erecting the building after 1837.

19. Quoted in Laura Fowler Woolworth: **Littleton Fowler, 1803-1846.** 1936, n.p., 9.

4

The Elusive
East Texas Border

by
Thomas F. Ruffin

Thomas F. Ruffin, Shreveport civic and business leader, has authored over fifty articles on early Louisiana and East Texas history. He has served as President of the North Louisiana Historical Association.

4

During its short life, the Republic of Texas was plagued with boundary problems with Mexico and also with the United States. One of the most troublesome spots was the north-south line that ran — or to be more accurate, supposedly ran — between the Red and Sabine Rivers in East Texas. In 1838, the Texas Secretary of State complained:

> The country through which the line will pass is now rapidly settling by an active and enterprizing population, whose condition is rendered unpleasant and embarassing [sic] by the uncertainty which exists in regard to the true boundary. While such a state of things continues this Government cannot enforce its revenue laws, neither can it make suitable preparations for the defence of that frontier . . .[1]

Confusion prevailed. Settlers, and even entire communities, had no way of determining whether they were in the United States or in the Republic of Texas. Red

River County, Texas found its territory being claimed by Miller County, Arkansas and to a lesser degree, Caddo Parish, Louisiana.

Only a joint survey of the boundary line by the two nations would resolve the many problems, but such was not forthcoming until 1841. In the meantime, the United States, on its own, surveyed the frontier extensively, claiming the area as American soil. But this only served to complicate matters. Many of those living on the surveyed lands continued to owe their allegiance to Texas, and one resident became a member of the Texas Congress.

Tempers flared occasionally, but only one military encounter developed. In November, 1838, the Texas Militia, under Major-General Thomas J. Rusk, crossed the border into Caddo Parish while pursuing a band of Indians. Briefly "occupying" Shreveport, the Texans almost precipitated a break in relations between the two nations.[2]

When the 1841 joint survey finally settled the boundary dispute, the Republic of Texas was the clear winner. Caddo Parish, Louisiana gave up over 450 square miles while Arkansas lost an entire county.

The boundary difficulties were not a recent development. Going back to the 1700s there had never been a clearly defined line separating Spanish Texas and French Louisiana. Later, when Texas and Louisiana were both under Spanish control, no boundary was necessary. When Louisiana reacquired Louisiana, it was to "the same extent that it now has in the hands of Spain, and that it had when France possessed it . . ."[3] The line was just as vague in 1803, when the United States purchased Louisiana.[4]

In 1804, the Louisiana Purchase was divided into two regions. That part north of the thirty-third parallel (which approximates the present Louisiana-Arkansas state line) became the Louisiana District; that part to the south, the Orleans Territory. The latter was "to extend west to the western boundary of said cession . . . ," a description which provided little clarification.[5] Hostilities appeared imminent along the border in 1806, but were averted when General James B. Wilkinson, the ranking officer in the American Army, and Lieutenant Colonel Simon De Herrera, in the service of the Spanish king, agreed on a "neutral zone" between the Rio (or Arroyo) Hondo — a short, non-descript stream near Natchitoches — and the Sabine River.[6]

The boundary question remained far from solution when the Orleans Territory became the State of Louisiana in 1812. Nevertheless, the new state proceeded to describe its western boundary as running along the **middle** of the Sabine River "to the thirty-second degree of north latitude — thence due north. . . ."[7] Although two Congressional Acts — the Enabling Act[8] and the Act of Admission[9] — acknowledged these same western limits, the United States continued to observe the neutral zone.

It was not until 1819 that Spain and the United States signed a treaty establishing the boundary. The line was to run along the **western** bank of the Sabine River "to the 32nd degree of latitude; thence, by a line due north to the degree of latitude where it strikes the Rio Roxo, of Natchitoches, or **Red River**. . . ."[10] As this new line was to run due north from the point where the thirty-second parallel hit the western bank rather than where it hit the middle of the Sabine River, it was relocated a few feet west of the boundary line originally claimed by the state of Louisiana. Moving an unmarked line, however, had little effect. Although the two nations had reached an agreement relative to this stretch of international boundary, a joint Spanish-American survey would be required to mark the actual line. A seemingly easy task, it was still not forthcoming.

The United States finally ratified the Treaty in 1821. The following year, the Americans established an army outpost, Cantonment Jesup, in the old neutral zone and began issuing land grants to settlers in the area. Before any steps could be taken toward marking the boundary line, however, the Mexicans had overthrown the Spaniards, setting up a republic of their own. This necessitated new negotiations and a new treaty. In 1828, the Mexican-American treaty was signed, recognizing the boundary of 1819, but once again, ratification of the treaty was delayed, this time until 1832.[11] Before Mexico and the United States got around to surveying the line, the Americans acquired a new neighbor to the west — the Republic of Texas. Once more it was back to the negotiating table.

In 1838, the United States and Texas held a Boundary Convention. The border established previously by Spain and the United States was again recognized. More important, however, definite steps were taken to survey the line.[12] By early 1840, the resulting Joint Commission had reached the mouth of the Sabine to begin its work. Their efforts were hampered by Martin Van Buren's contention that the "Sabine River" referred to in the treaties was, in reality, the Neches River that likewise flowed into Sabine Lake. Once this and other differences were reconciled, the Commission proceeded north, surveying the western bank of the Sabine River. Reaching Logan's Ferry (today's Logansport), then in Caddo Parish, later that year, they decided to delay further surveying temporarily because of unfavorable climatic conditions.[13]

Before reviewing the results of this joint survey, it might be well to take a brief look at earlier American attempts to plot the region.

The United States retained title to all vacant lands in the Louisiana Purchase. For this acreage to be properly identified before being sold or given away, it had to be properly surveyed. A novel and rather simple method was developed by Thomas Hutchins, Geographer to the United States. First used in Ohio in 1785, it has since been used in all public-land states and has been adopted by several foreign countries.[14] His system consisted of laying out square townships, six miles to a side. Wherever possible, the townships were then subdivided into 36 sections, each one mile square and containg 640 acres:

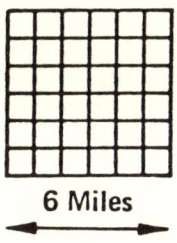

6 Miles

The townships were laid out in grid fashion, beginning at the intersection of an east-west Base Line and a north-south Meridian. The townships would then be identified according to their location; the number of Townships north (or south) of the Base Line; the number of Ranges east (or west) of the Meridian. Thus, the shaded township below would be referred to as Township 2 North, Range 4 West — or more simply, T2N, R4W:

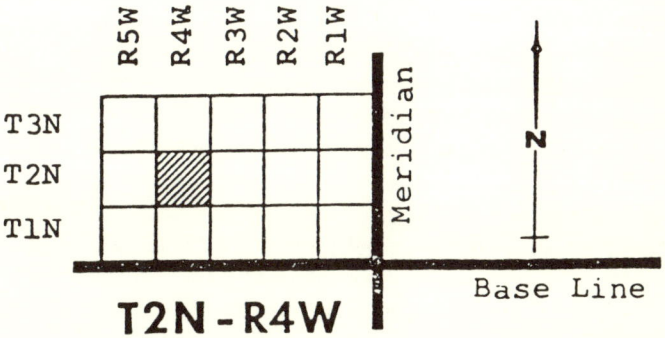

T2N - R4W

By 1807, the United States Government had extended the existing St. Stephens Base Line along the thirty-first parallel. At the same time, the Louisiana Meridian was laid out, intersecting the Base Line about 18 miles south of Alexandria. It was from this point that the surveying of townships began in the Territory of Orleans.[15]

Surveying progressed rapidly in the southern part of the Territory, even before Louisiana attained statehood in 1812. Very little could take place in the northwestern section until after the Treaty of 1819 had been ratified in 1821. Before that time, the United States had no true idea of their western limits. Afterwards, the surveyors knew exactly how far west they could go — at least, south of the thirty-second parallel, where the Sabine River served as the border. All of the old neutral zone ended up as American soil. By November 1824, the Register and Receiver of the United States Land Office in Opelousas was able to report to the Secretary of the Treasury on some 280 claims. These were filed by settlers "in the late neutral territory" and were based on "habitation, occupancy, and cultivation on and previous to the 22nd of February, 1819."[16] All except 69 of the claims were recommended for approval, most for 640 acres.[17] So these grants could be readily identified, much of the area between the Rio Hondo and the Sabine River was surveyed by 1830.[18]

The extreme northwestern corner of Louisiana still faced other difficulties. North of the thirty-second parallel, the border no longer followed the Sabine. Rather, it followed a line that had yet to be drawn. In addition, this section was the private domain of the Caddo Indians. As such, it was not occupied by whites. All of this changed in 1835 when the Caddoes conveyed their lands[19] to the United States. As for the vague western boundary, it was described in the treaty as "the north and south line which separates the United States from Mexico, wheresoever the same shall be defined and acknowledged by the two governments."[20]

The Caddo's old lands were very desirable. With the removal of the Great Raft on Red River, the area also became quite accessible. By 1837, the Shreve Town Company began selling town lots in the new community of Shreveport. The following year, sufficient people had moved into the region to justify the creation of a new parish, Caddo. Caddo Parish's western limits were to pursue "the boundary line of the United States and Louisiana" — and to acquire the accompanying problems.

The settlers continued to arrive and so did the surveyors, who were soon subdividing Caddo Parish into townships and sections. However, they were faced with an immediate problem. With an unmarked boundary line, they had to decide how far west to go. It was soon resolved that the United States would survey to the western line of Range 17 West. (See Map A)

Between January, 1837, and January, 1838, H. T. Williams, the federal government's Surveyor General of Louisiana, signed contracts calling for surveys of all townships in the two westernmost ranges, 16 West and 17 West. By the end of 1839, all work on both township and section lines had been completed.[22] The United States assumed jurisdiction over the area, if only by implication, as did Louisiana and Caddo Parish. Just how effective such control may have been remains doubtful. There were many settlers who felt that they lived in Texas no matter where the Americans placed the line. Among these was the outspoken Colonel Robert Potter, whose home on Potter's Point was located in Township 20 North, Range 17 West[23] — at least, according to the United States survey teams. Undaunted, he ran for, and was elected to, the Congress of the Republic of Texas.[24]

There were other settlers, it might be added, who took full advantage of the vague boundary by showing no loyalty to either country.

Although a number of colonists lived along the frontier, the surveyor indicated only a handful of cultivated fields in Ranges 16 and 17 West. On what would later become Texas soil, they noted a mere dozen or so, identifying most of them.[25] In contrast, they found five Indian villages in the two ranges. One was south of Greenwood;[26] two, just north of today's Waskom, and two more near Potter's Point.[27] Although Texas was plagued with

Map A:
By the time the Texas-U.S. boundary was pinpointed in 1841, Federal surveyors had already laid out numerous townships along the frontier. To the settlers, this strongly suggested that the Americans were assuming jurisdiction over the area. Indian villages found by those surveyors are identified by stars.

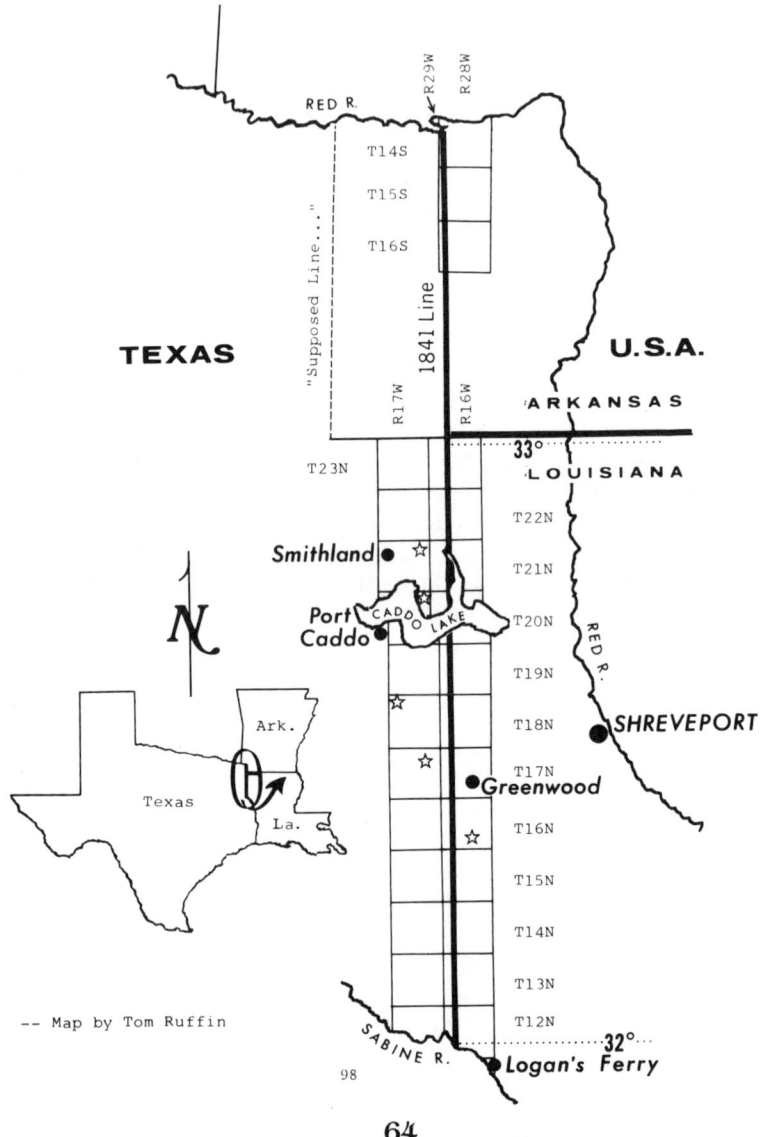

-- Map by Tom Ruffin

Indian trouble, the close proximity of the red man had little effect on life along the border.

The surveyors resolved the fate of one community, Port Caddo. Shown on some earlier maps as being in Louisiana,[28] it ended up just west of Range 17 west and thus beyond the limits of the American survey. The future Greenwood in Range 16, West, however, remained hazy. Passing through the latter community in late 1840, traveller Adolphus Sterne recorded in his diary: "the place is in a Languid state, in consequence of the belief that the place will be in the Limits of Texas, in fact all inhabitants are fearfull [sic] they will be in Texas after the line is run. . . ."[29] Another village that later cropped up in the surveyed area was Smithland.[30]

Whatever the Americans hoped to gain from a unilateral survey of the Louisiana-Texas frontier, they failed to accomplish it. Confusion spread as more and more settlers arrived in the area. It became increasingly urgent to establish the border line by a bilateral survey, thereby removing all doubts as to its true location. Meanwhile, in Arkansas, federal surveyors were running into similar problems along the frontier.

Arkansas was part of the original Louisiana District, which was renamed the Louisiana Territory, and later, the Missouri Territory. Then, in 1819, an area approximating the present states of Oklahoma (minus the panhandle) and Arkansas became the Arkansaw [sic] Territory. With cessions to the Indians, Congress kept moving Arkansas' western boundary eastward until it reached its current location in 1828. Except for a minor adjustment near Fort Smith several years later, the line North of the Red River had been resolved.[31] South of the river, however, the story was different. Although the boundary description had been spelled out by Congress in 1828,[32] the line's exact location still remained locally in doubt when Arkansas attained statehood in 1836.[33]

This created many problems for Texans, particulary those living in Red River County in the northeastern corner of the Republic. The county would soon encounter difficulties with Louisiana because of the poorly defined border, but this proved to be minor in comparison with its troubles with Arkansas. The Texas Congress, when creating Red River County in 1837, used this description:

> Beginning at the mouth of the Bois d'Arc, running up that stream to Carter Cliffs, crossing thence south to a point west to the head of Bid [Big] Cypress, east to its head, down that to Sodo Lake, thence east to the line of the United States, with that line to Red River, up that to the beginning.[34]

The conflict was with old Miller County, a fascinating carry-over from the Territory to the State of Arkansas.[35] Originally covering much of today's southern Oklahoma, the county had to move as its lands were ceded to the Choctaws. Thus, during the mid-twenties, Miller County reluctantly relocated south of the Red River, claiming this area:

> Beginning at the south bank of the Red River, at a point due south of mouth of the Cositot; thence due south to the thirty-third degree of north latitude; thence due west with the thirty-third degree of north latitude to a point south of the Faux-ouachita [the False Ouachita, or Washita, in today's Oklahoma], thence to Red River; thence down and with said river to the place of beginning.[36]

Not only did Red River County, Texas and Miller County, Arkansas overlap, they virtually claimed the same territory. (See Map B) Even their county seats, Clarksville and Jonesborough, were a mere 25 miles apart. Neighbors, and even friends and relatives, had divided loyalties. The resulting situation was quite chaotic.[37]

Although the State of Arkansas may have envisioned a western empire, the United States surveyors failed to share their enthusiasm. They never got around to surveying Miller County.

Federal surveying in Arkansas began in 1815 when the Fifth Principal Meridian and Base Line were established, intersecting about 25 miles west of Helena. It was from this point that much of what was then the Missouri Territory was surveyed.[38] In southern Arkansas,

Map B:
Adding to the frontier difficulties were the overlapping boundaries of Red River County, Tewas; Miller County, Arkansas; and Caddo Parish, Louisiana. Conflicting authority hampered the settlers.

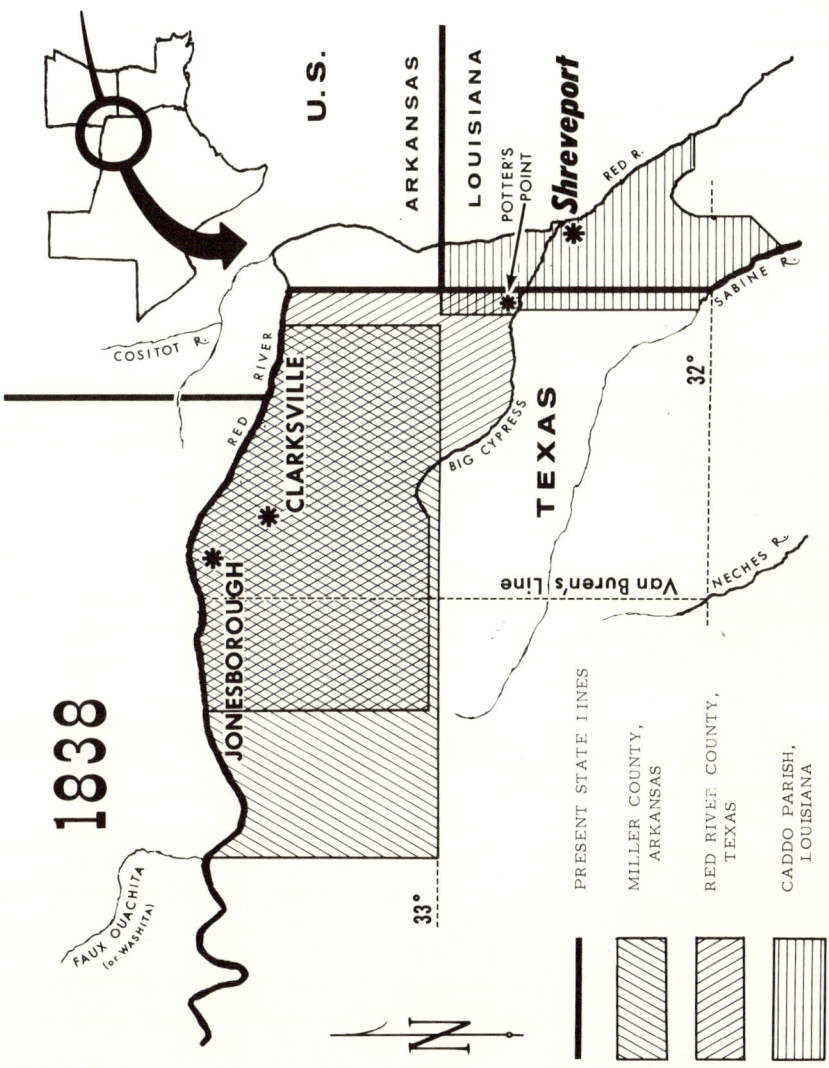

the surveyors reached the Red River in the mid 1820s, but were reluctant to cross it — and did not do so until years later.[39] In fact, it was not until 1840 that David Fulton, the federal government's Surveyor of Public Lands in Arkansas, reported to the Commissioner General of the U. S. Land Office that he "had sent out three efficient surveyors, one of whom has taken a contract to survey exteriors [i.e., the township lines as opposed to the section lines] south of the Red River . . . The survey of **ten townships** there, will . . . be completed during the winter."[40]

Along with his report, Fulton included a map showing the progress of surveys in Arkansas up to that time. The region southwest of Red River, devoid of any surveying activity, was designated "Disputed Territory." (See Map A) He drew a line, however, south along the range line between Ranges 30 and 31 West, labeling it the "Supposed line between the United States and Texas"[41] — which was a long way east of Jonesborough and the center of Miller County activity. By design or coincidence, his line struck the thirty-third parallel about five miles west of the western limits assumed by the federal surveyors in Louisiana.[42]

The approach of the surveyors in the two states was quite different. In Louisiana, they expressed little doubt as to the probable location of the boundary and quickly surveyed to that point, completing their work by 1839. In contrast, their counterparts in Arkansas moved quite cautiously, never surveying as far west as the Louisiana surveyors. As it developed, the Arkansas surveyors did not even begin work in Range 28 West until late 1840. By early 1841, they substantially completed their work in three townships — 14, 15, and 16 South — in that Range as well as a small portion of Township 14 South, Range 29 West that ended up in a bend of the river.[43] As events would prove later that year, the Arkansas surveyors had barely reached the border.

It was mid-February, 1841, when the members of the Joint Commission returned to their encampment near Logan's Ferry. The Texans were headed by their commissioner, Memucan Hunt; the Americans by their commissioner, John H. Overton. High water and other difficulties hampered the party considerably. In fact, two months elapsed before they were able to pin-point the exact spot at which the thirty-second parallel crossed the Western bank of the Sabine River. Even then, they were unable to mark the location. So, on April 23, the party erected a granite marker on the boundary meridan two miles, 1988.5 feet north of the parallel.[44] From there, the group moved northward, covering one, two, and sometimes more miles per day. At each mile, they built a dirt mound five feet high.[45] (See Map C).

Crossing section lines marked off earlier by the federal surveyors, the Joint Commission readily realized that they were east of the western limits of the United States survey. Near the fifth mound, they found just how far. Their "boundary line (was) 3,763 feet east of the range line dividing the 16 and 17th ranges" — or about 6-3/4 miles east of the western line of Range 17 West.[46] In other words, one entire range (17 West) plus a small slice of another (16 West) had been incorrectly assumed to be a part of the United States. On subsequent checks south of Caddo Lake, the distances varied somewhat, but always exceeded 6-1/2 miles.[47] North of the lake, the range lines are one mile further to the west. Hence the boundary line between the lake and the thirty-third parallel was about 1-1/2 miles east of the range line between Ranges 16 and 17 West — and about 7-1/2 miles east of the point to which the United States had originally surveyed in 1837-39.[48]

For the first time settlers knew on which side of the line they lived. Some found themselves in Louisiana. Others, such as Robert Potter, found that they were indeed Texans. (See Map D) And Potter could continue serving in the Texas Congress until his untimely death in the Regulators-Moderators War the following year.[49] Smithland discovered that it was in Texas; Greenwood, in Louisiana. Caddo Parish — and at the same time, Louisiana and the United States — lost a strip 70 miles long and from 6-1/2 to 7-1/2 miles wide to the Republic of Texas.

Map C:
Here are the first 36 miles of the Texas-U.S. border as established by the Joint Commission in 1841. This line was about 6½ miles east of the western edge of Range 17 West, the point to which American surveyors had surveyed earlier.

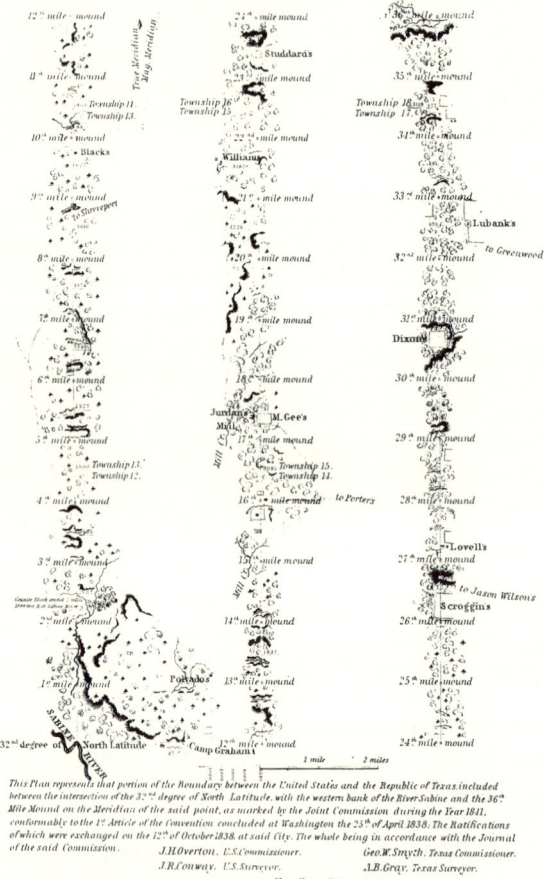

Paradoxically, as one boundary dispute was settled, another was created. On June 5, 1841, the Joint Commission marked the location of the thirty-third parallel — 1,692 feet north of the 69th mound — and erected a marker there.[50] Unfortunately this parallel, which separated Arkansas from Louisiana, had previously been placed about 3,205 feet further north — or just south of where the 70th mound was erected.[51] This new border problem was not resolved until 1895, when the western six miles of the Arkansas-Louisiana border was surveyed along the original line.[52]

Proceeding north into Arkansas, the Joint Commission was hit by illness — but they continued to push through "an almost unpenetratable undergrowth of young oaks and hickory." The group found that the first few miles had not yet been covered by the United States surveyors. It was not until they reached the 90th mound that the party encountered the first township line of the Arkansas survey — 1,984 feet east of the range line that served as the western limits of the Arkansas survey southwest of Red River.[53] This was, however, about 12-½ miles east of the unmarked "Supposed line between the United States and Texas" that appeared in David Fulton's 1840 map.

Arkansas townships were laid out at a slight angle from true north. Thus the range line and the new boundary line closed in on each other as they stretched northward. By the time the two lines reached the Red River, they were a mere 162 feet apart.[54] In contrast to the large amount of surveyed lands lost in Louisiana, Arkansas (and Lafayette County) lost very little — just a narrow strip 18 miles long with an average width of about 1,073 feet. Worse though, no part of Miller County ended up within the State of Arkansas. The entire country found itself within the boundaries of Texas.[55] Thus old Miller County's short, illustrious history came to an abrupt end.[56]

As to the effects on the colonists in the area, United States Commissioner John H. Overton made these observations in his report to the Secretary of State, Daniel Webster:

Map D:
Robert Potter — who served Texas as Secretary of the Navy, signer of the new republic's Declaration of Independence and Constitution, and a member of Congress — was caught on the frontier controversy. The Americans surveyed westward to Line A, indicating that Potter's home on Potter's Point was in the United States. The 1841 boundary, however, was placed along Line B, affirming that he indeed was domiciled in the Republic of Texas.

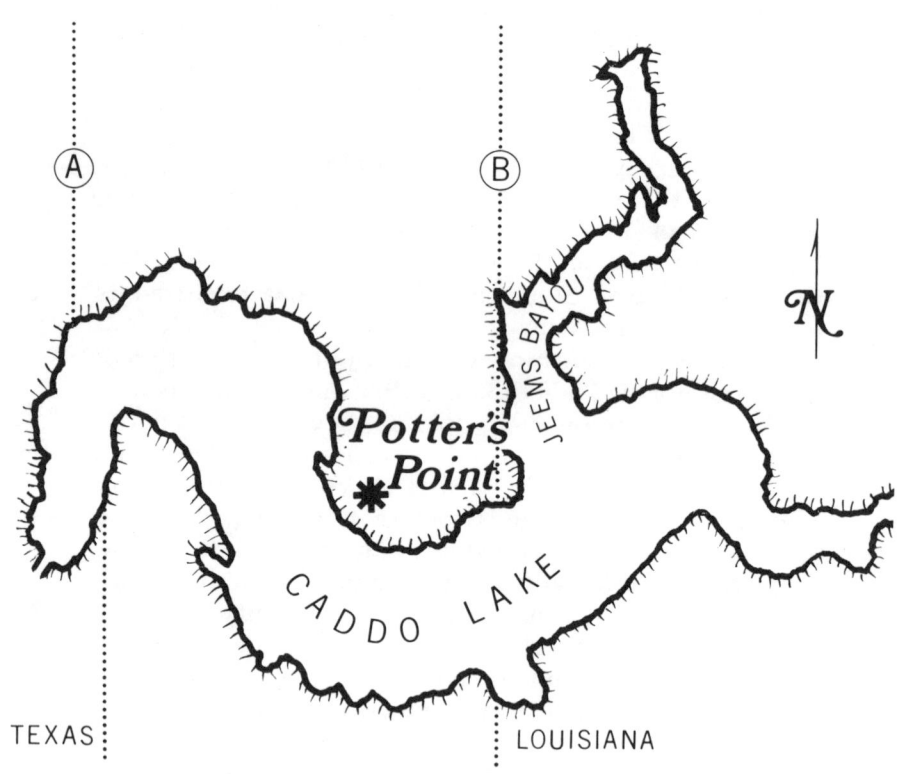

As defined and marked, it leaves the western bank of the Sabine River, according to the first measurement I was enabled to have made in connection with the survey of public lands in the State of Louisiana, north of the 32nd parallel, 3,763 feet east of the line dividing ranges 16 and 17, at lake Soda, or Ferry Lake, 46 miles north, 2,840 feet east, and at its termination on the Red River, 162 feet east of the dividing line between ranges 28 and 29 of the United States survey in the State of Arkansas.

Although about half of the western range of sections in the 16th range of townships, and the entire seventeenth range of townships in the State of Louisiana, have fallen, by the determination of the boundary, within the limits of the republic of Texas, yet the interests of the settler, with a few exceptions, have not been prejudiced. The fostering policy of the neighboring Government had, in anticipation of such a result, liberly provided for, by donations of land to the actual settler and cultivator. The exceptions alluded to are not numerous. They are those claiming under purchase from the United States, whose improvements have been served by the course of the line, thereby rendering measurably valueless the portion left them. The reimbursement of the purchase money, as in ordinary cases, would not, I am induced to believe, indemnify them for the loss they have sustained, and I therefore, **at their earnest solicitation,** beg leave, through your Department, to present to the President the consideration of their cases.

The limits of the State of Arkansas, between the 33rd degree of latitude and the Red River, had no other determinate bounds, I believe; than those recognised and temporarily secured by the provisions of the convention; and her jurisdiction west of the established boundry, like that of Louisiana over the 17th range of townships, had been recent, and generally considered of doubtful title. Hence, the inhabitants, along the whole extent of this frontier, evidenced neither disappointment nor dissatisfaction in the change of relations produced by the settlement of the limits. As a neighboring class of population, identical in language, manners, and institutions, and more than ordinarily distinguished for intelligence, enterprise, and industry, they will more than counterbalance for any loss of territory, in the mutual protection and safety they will assuredly afford to those frontiers, by the continuous cultivation of those friendly relations which have heretofore existed.[57]

After Texas joined the Union in 1845, the new line no longer remained an international boundary. During the years that followed, the line has served as the border between Texas on the west and Arkansas and Louisiana on the east — as sister states in both the United States and the Confederacy. The line's location remains unchanged, although there has been at least one attempt to tamper with it. In 1941, Bascom Giles, Commissioner of the General Land Office of Texas, suggested that the line be moved 150 feet to the east.[58] But so far, no serious steps have been taken toward accomplishing this end.[59]

Texas almost became a public-land state with the federal government's holding title to all public land.[60] Had this been done, Texas would have utilized the same "township and range" surveying system used by Louisiana, Arkansas, and other western states. As it developed, Texas was permitted to retain all public lands within its borders.[61] Over the years, millions of these acres were granted to Texas war veterans, immigrants, and others. Once a warrant was issued by the government, the holder would select his alloted acreage from any vacant, unappropriated lands.[62] By necessity, some of the resulting grants were odd-shaped.

Many grants were for 640 acres,[63] the number of acres included in a section surveyed by the United States government. When Texas was able to claim additional land along the Louisiana border in 1841, it had already been laid out in townships and sections by the Americans. If there was ever a tailor-made situation, this was it: unappropriated public land already marked off with the exact number of acres, just waiting to be selected by a claimant.

Many took advantage of these circumstances, particularly in Harrison County. Here a large number of 640 acre grants were made of the same dimensions and in the same location as the sections previously surveyed by the Americans.[64] There are still further instances of different size grants, where one or more sides utilized the old section lines.[65] Even Robert Potter, in his will and in an 1842 deed, found it expedient to use descriptions based on the United States survey.[66]

Rather than having one uniform survey prepared by government surveyors, East Texas relied on many independent surveyors whose work had to be pieced to-

Map E:
This area of Harrison County, Texas was encompassed in Township 18 North, Range 17 West of the Louisiana Survey. Here is how that township looks when superimposed on the Texas General Land Office Map. Note how many section lines were retained without change. (Note the location of mounds along the border.)

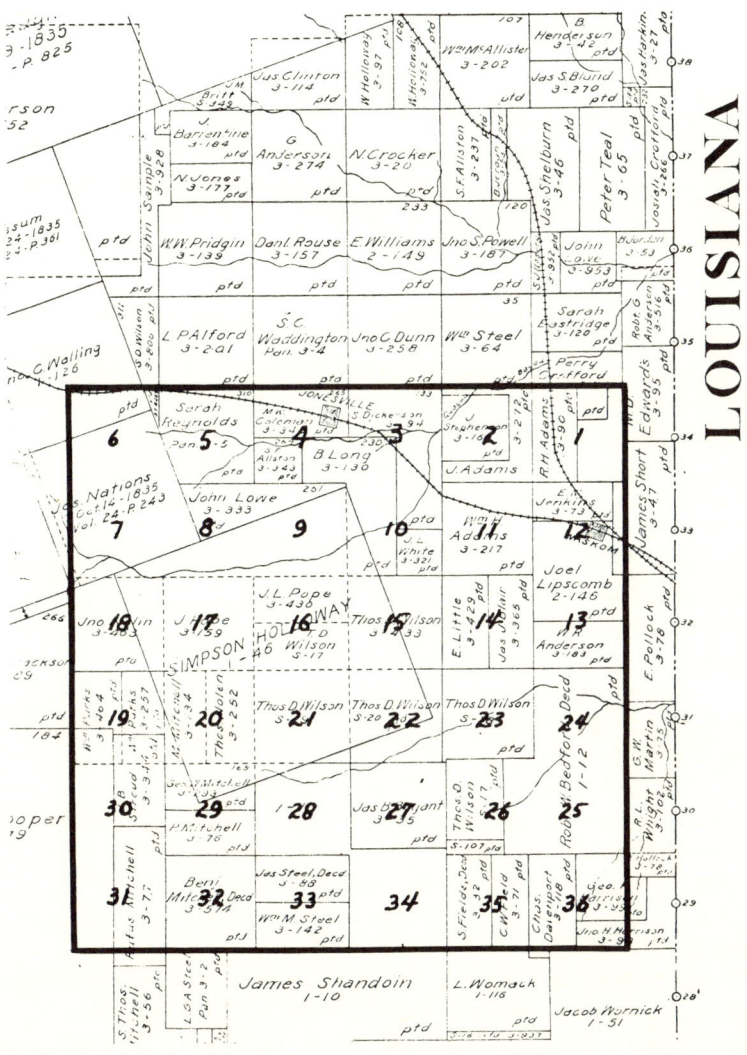

gether like a jigsaw puzzle. One notable exception to this patch-work quilt effect is in the area acquired from Louisiana.[67] Here, based on the earlier American surveys, the north-south and east-west property lines still prevail. (See Map E)

Notes

1. Letter from Dr. Robert A. Irion to Hon. Alcee LaBranch, Charge d'Affaires of the U.S., February 13, 1838. George Pierce Garrison (ed.), **Diplomatic Correspondence of the Republic of Texas**, in **Annual Report of the American Historical Association for the Year 1907**, (2 vols., Washington, D.C., 1908), II, Part I, 291-296.

2. Thomas F. Ruffin, "Invasion of Caddo Parish by General Thomas Jefferson Rusk's Republic of Texas Army, 1838," **North Louisiana Historical Association Journal**, II, (Spring 1971), 71-83.

3. Treaty of San Ildefonso, signed October 1, 1800, quoted from Louisiana Purchase Treaty, 8 U.S. **Statutes at Large**, 200.

4. Treaty between the United States of America and the French Republic (often referred to as the Louisiana Purchase Treaty); signed April 30, 1803, proclaimed October 21, 1803, 8 Stat. 200.

5. 2 Stat. 283; Proclaimed March 26, 1804.

6. "The Neutral Ground Agreement" in Ernest Wallace and David M. Vigness (eds.), **Documents of Texas History** (Austin, Texas, 1963), 37-38.

7. Preamble to The **Constitution of the State of Louisiana**, 1812.

8. 2 Stat. 641; proclaimed February 20, 1811.

9. 2 Stat. 701; proclaimed April 8, 1812. Limits of the state were enlarged a few days later with the addition of the "Florida Parishes," but this did not affect Louisiana's western border.

10. Treaty of Amity, Settlement, and Limits, between the United States of America and His Catholic Majesty (often referred to as the Treaty of 1819 or the Adams-Onis Treaty), signed February 22, 1819, proclaimed February 19, 1821; 8 Stat. 252.

11. Treaty of Limits between the United States and the United Mexican States signed January 12, 1828, proclaimed April 5, 1832; 8 Stat, 372.

12. Boundary Convention between the United States and the Republic of Texas; signed April 5, 1832, proclaimed October 13, 1838; 8 Stat. 511.

13. Thomas Maitland Marshall, **A History of the Western Boundary of the Louisiana Purchase, 1819-1841** (Berkeley, Calif., 1914), 225-238.

14. Hilde Heun Kagan, et al (eds.), The American Heritage Pictorial Atlas of the United States (New York, 1966) 126. Franklin K. Van Zandt, Boundaries of the United States and the Several States, Geological Survey Bulletin 1212 (Washington, D.C., 1966), 129.

15. At least west of the Mississippi River. The same Base Line, but another meridian (the St. Helena) was used for the Orleans Territory east of the river.

16. Quoted from printed affadavit forms used for filing "Rio Hondo" claims. Originals on file at the Louisiana State Land Office, Baton Rouge, La. February 22, 1819 represents the date that the treaty of 1819 was signed.

17. U.S., 19th Congress, 1st Session, House Document 50.

18. U.S. Government Township Plats for townships in Sabine, Natchitoches, and De Soto parishes; originals on file at Louisiana State Land Office.

19. The Caddo lands approximated present-day Miller County, Ark. and Caddo Parish, La.

20. Caddo Indian Treaty; signed May 30, 1835, proclaimed January 26, 1836; U.S. 27th Congress, 2d Session, House Rep. No. 1035, 73-78.

21. Act No. 67 of 1838: "to create and establish the parish of Cado (sic) and for other purposes," approved January 18, 1838, Louisiana Legislative Acts, 1838, 11-13.

22. U.S. Government Township Plat, townships in Ranges 16 and 17 West (La. Mer.). Originals on file at Louisiana State Library; photostats on file at Texas State Library, Austin, Texas. T12N, R17W was surveyed, but never plated.

23. U.S. Government Township Plat, T20N, R17W (La. Mer.). Original on file at Louisiana State Land Office.

24. For an account of Robert Potter, his wife and family, see the historical novel by Edith Hamilton Kirkland, Love Is a Wild Assault (New York, 1959). Potter, it might be added, had previously served as Secretary of the Navy for Texas and had been instrumental in the preparation of both the Texas Declaration of Independence and the Texas Constitution. Also see: The History of Harriet A. Ames during the Early Days of Texas. Written by Herself at the Age of Eighty-Three. Genealogy Collection, Shreve Memorial Library, Shreveport, Louisiana.

25. In addition to Col. Potter, the surveyors mentioned Moore, Davis, Johnson, (Amos) Johnson, (Thomas S.) Wilson, (Vashti) Gibbs, Warmack, and Shad Owen (undoubtedly James Shandoin). U.S. Government Township Plats, townships in Range 17 West (La. Mar.); originals on file at Louisiana State Land Office. Probable first names from Texas General Land Office Map of Harrison County, Map of Panola County, and Map of the Marion County; originals on file at the Texas General Land Office, Austin, Texas.

26. U.S. Government Township Plat, T16N, R16W (La. Mer.); original on file at Louisiana State Land Office.

27. U.S. Government Township Plats, T17N, R17W; T20N, R20W, and T21N, R17W (La. Mer.); originals on file at Louisiana State Land Office. Kirkland, Love is a Wild Assault described relations with nearby Indians.

28. One such map was the "Map of Texas compiled from surveys recorded in the Land Office of the Republic of Texas and other official surveys," by John Arrowsmith (London, England, 1841); original at Texas State Library, file No. 438.

29. Harriet Smithers (ed.), "Diary of Adophus Sterne" in **Southwestern Historical Quarterly**, XXXI (July 1927), 76-77.

30. Another traveller visiting the frontier was Josiah Gregg in 1841. He found Smithland "unhealthy," but Greenwood "healthful." Maurice Garland Fulton (ed.), Josiah Gregg, **Diary & Letters of Josiah Gregg**, (2 vols; Norman, Olka., 1941), I, 87, 118.

31. Van Zandt, **Boundaries of the United States and the Several States**, 191-194.

32. ". . . running due west on that (33rd) parallel of latitude, to where a line running due north from latitude thirty-two degrees north, on the Sabine River, will intersect with the same. . . ." 4 Stat. 276.

33. The enabling act for Arkansas statehood, proclaimed June 15, 1836, described the line in this area as "bounded on the south side of Red River by the Mexican boundary line to the northwest corner of the State of Louisiana." 5 Stat. 50.

34. "An act to define the boundaries of the county of Red River," approved December 18, 1837; H. P. N. Gammel, **The Laws of Texas, 1822-1897** (Austin, Texass, 1898), II, 89-90. The description "Sodo Lake" was often used interchangeabley with "Caddo Lake" or "Ferry Lake," and undoubtedly was in this instance. Sodo Lake was entirely within the boundaries of Louisiana, while Caddo, or Ferry, Lake straddled the border line.

35. Miller County, Arkansas Territory was created April 1, 1820 from Hempstead County; Dallas T. Herndon (ed.), **Annals of Arkansas**, (Hopkinsville, Ky., 1947), 699. Old Miller County should not be confused with the present Miller County, which was not established until many years later.

36. Act of Nov. 3, 1831; Ibid., 699.

37. The history of old Miller County is a fascinating one, but too long to be adequately covered here. See John Hugh Reynolds, "The Western Boundary of Arkansas" in **Arkansas Historical Association Publications** II (1908), 211-236; Rex W. Strickland, "Miller County, Arkansas Territory: The Frontier That Men Forgot" in **Chronicles of Oklahoma**, XVIII (March 1940), 12-14, (June 1940), 154-170; and XIX (March 1941) 37-54; and Tom Ruffin, "Lost County of the Ark-La-Tex" in **Shreveport Magazine**, XXV (September 1970), 22 ff.

38. A marker near the site indicates that it was the point "from which the lands of the Louisiana Purchase were surveyed." Much of the Purchase — four complete states and parts of two others — were surveyed from the 5th Principal Meridian and this Base Line. The balance of the Louisiana Purchase, however, including the State of Louisiana, used other Meridians and Base Lines.

39. T20S, R26W (5th Pr. Mer.) east of Red River was surveyed in 1823; that part of the township west of the river was not surveyed until 1841. U.S. Government Township Plat, T20S, R26W (5th Pr. Mer.); original on file at the Arkansas Land Office, Little Rock, Arkansas.

40. U.S., 26th Congress 2d Session, Senate Document 61, 110.

41. Ibid., map opposite p. 112.

42. The Fifth Principal Meridian was established independently of the Louisiana Meridian. Thus the Arkansas and Louisiana Range numbers do not correspond. For example, R26W in Arkansas almost aligns itself with R14W in Louisiana.

43. U.S. Government Township Plats, T14S, R28W & R29W; T15S; R28W; and T16S, R28W (5th Pr Mer.); original on file at Arkansas Land Office.

44. "Journal of the Joint Commission" in U.S., **27th Congress, 2d Session, House Document 51**, 68-71. The marker was engraved "meridian boundary, established A.D. 1841" on the south side; "U.S." on the east side; and "R.T." on the west side.

45. "Journal on the Joint Commission," Ibid., 72-73, 72n. The "Journal" also appeared in U.S., **27th Congress, 2d Session, Senate Document 199**, but all quotations and page numbers used here are from the House version. For background, see Marshall, **A History of the Western Boundary of the Louisiana Purchase, 1819-1941**, 225-241.

46. "Journal of the Joint Commission," 72.

47. Other measurements taken near the 10th, 20th, 38th, and 45th mounds. **Ibid.**, 73-75.

48. One mile plus 2,635 feet near the 52nd mound; one mile plus 2,574 feet near the 55th mound; Ibid., 75.

49. Potter died on March 2, 1842 — on the sixth anniversary of the signing of the Texas Declaration of Independence. He served the area in the fifth and sixth congresses.

50. "Journal of the Joint Commission," 76.

51. U.S. Government Township Plat, T20S, R28W (5th Pr. Mer.) shows the original Arkansas-Louisiana boundary line to be 5.80 chains (or 382.8 feet) south of the 70th mound. Original on file at Arkansas Land Office.

52. Van Zandt, **Boundaries of the United States and the Several States**, 173. Also see: **Diagram in T23N, R16W** (La. Mer.) dated 9/12/91; **Diagram in T23N, R16W** (La. Mer.) dated 12/31/95; and **Diagram in T23N, R15W** (La. Mer.) dated 12/31/95; originals on file in Louisiana State Land Office.

53. "Journal of the Joint Commission," 76-77.

54. The distance between the range line (the western line of R28W) and the new boundary was 1,150 feet near the 90th mound, 820 feet near the 100th mound; **Ibid.**, 77-78.

55. Gammel, **The Laws of Texas**, I:83 (Approved February 3, 1844).

56. In 1874, a new Miller County was created; this time entirely within the boundaries of Arkansas. It covers that part of the state south and west of Red River.

57. Letter from John J. Overton to Hon. Daniel Webster, Secretary of State of the U.S., August 10, 1841; U.S., **27th Congress, 2d Session, House Document 51,** 59-60.

58. Letter from Bascom Giles to Hon. Sam Jones, Governor of Louisiana, November 25, 1941; **Reply Brief, Texas vs. Louisiana,** No. 36 Original in the Supreme Court of the United States (October Term 1970), 96-101. The 150 feet represents the distance between a line drawn north from where the thirty-second parallel hits the western bank of the Sabine and a line drawn north from where that parallel hits the center of the river.

59. The suit recently filed by Texas against Louisiana — No. 36 Original in the Supreme Court of the United States (October Term 1970) — involved only the disputed ownership of the western half of the Sabine River. The land portion of the boundary north of the thirty-second parallel was not included.

60. A Texas-U.S. treaty, signed April 12, 1844, but rejected by the U.S. Senate, provided in Article IV: "The public lands hereby ceded shall be subject to laws regulating public lands in other territories of the United States . . ."; Wallace and Vigness, **Documents of Texas,** 143-144.

61. The U.S. Senate Resolution authorizing the annexation of Texas (5 Stat. 97), proclaimed March 1, 1845 provided that the new state "shall also retain all vacant and unappropriate lands lying within its limits."

62. The generally accepted figure for headright, bounty, and donation grants is 36,876,492 acres, but this is far from accurate. Thomas L. Miller, "Texas Bounty Land Grants, 1835-1888" in Southwestern Historical Quarterly, LXVI (October 1962), 222.

63. John Burlage and J. E. Hollingsworth, **Abstract of Valid Land Claims, Compiled from the Records of the General Land Office and Court of Claims, of the State of Texas** (Austin, Texas, 1859), III-VIII, lists in simplified form the types of certificates issued, and the acreage generally involved.

64. **Harrison County Survey Record Books,** Clerk of Court's Office, Harrison County Court House, Marshall, Texas. The American surveyors used a chain of 66.00 feet for measurement, 80.00 being required per mile. Early Texas surveyors, on the other hand, relied on a vara of 33-1/3 inches, 1900.8 required per mile. In the United States survey, very few sections ended up measuring 80.00 chains, or one mile, per side. Yet, most of the Texas plats for these same 640 acres plots indicated four equal sides of exactly 1900 varas each — with no variation. It would appear that the early East Texas surveyors utilized the survey stakes placed by the Americans, without taking the time or the trouble to remeasure and verify the true distances.

5

River People

by
William Seale

William Seale lives and works in Virginia. He formerly taught at Lamar University, and is the author of **Texas Riverman, The Life and Times of Captain Andrew Smyth.**

5

The riverman, as an early Texas character, is virtually dead. He is not one of the popular frontier "types" around which we Texans like to base our vision of the past. The cattleman — the cotton planter — the lawyer — the sheriff — the Indian fighter — and the outlaw are all familiar sterotypes, and in our minds we have no trouble placing them in the streets of 1850 Galveston or 1840 Nacogdoches or at Washington-on-the-Brazos that spring of 1836. General Sam Houston pleases us mightily, because he was a lawyer, a sometimes cattleman, an Indian fighter; he had a mysterious past, and he was the hero of San Jacinto; Sam Houston epitomizes our concept of the early Texan, and we follow his career like fascinated movie fans, gobbling new manuscript material about him, reading undocumented books which dangle sensationally intimate fiction from bare threads of truth. River people lived in that world of Sam Houston and Three Legged Willie and Stephen F. Austin. Their lives were not particularly glamorous. Their purpose on the Texas scene is difficult for us to imagine.

There was a time when a man did not think it strange to address a letter, "Texas, In the Western Woods."[1] Indeed, the Texas people knew about, with relation to settlement, was just that: a great, silent woods. Land was not hard to get, in the midst of those woods. Accessible land, however, was quite another matter. The previous frontier experience had taught settlers that to realize dreams of riches, land was simply not enough. Texas cotton and corn and tobacco had to be sold; they had to be taken to market, and the best market was usually on the Gulf Coast. Roads were a great problem. New roads were stump-scattered and eroding — old roads were deep-rutted and muddy. Creeks and rivers were not bridged, and when a ferry was not available, one had either to build a raft or wait until the water level was low enough to facilitate crossing. Such a journey from San Augustine to Sabine Pass could take as much or more than six weeks. And too, land travelers risked the danger of damage to their wagon-cargo, and of course trouble with Indians and outlaws, which oddly, seemed to be the least of their worries.

River travel as the solution to the transportation need was not earth-shaking. Early Texans had traveled rivers before — the Tennessee, the Mississippi, the Fear, the Rappahannock. The problem was — "Who will be the rivermen?" Most people came to Texas to plant the land, to fulfill within themselves the agricultural ideal which dazzled nineteenth-century Americans. For everyone there existed the chance to reach this ideal, especially in the great uncleared, unplowed forests of Texas. Few settlers were willing to surrender their chances with the land for a life on the rivers. Consequently, as late as 1840, farmers laced their letters with mournful complaints about transportation, which, when it existed, was not in sufficient supply to fill the demand.[2]

Texas was not blessed with outstanding rivers. The Sabine, the Neches, the Trinity, the Colorado, and the Brazos were the pertinent streams where river travel was concerned. These rivers existed in an unimproved state through the Mexican years, the Republic, and in fact, until well after the Civil War. Narrow and twisting, the rivers were sometimes so shallow in their natural state that rivermen had to await the spring rise before they could hope to reach their destination. Sunken logs, fallen as trees from the riverbank, slanted upward from the bottom of the river, and lurked just beneath the surface as "snags," water-seasoned to rock hardness, so firmly secured in their positions that they could rip a boat in half as it pressed upon them in the current. Rock shoals and sandbars were hidden in the dark waters, threatening damage and chaos to vessels; the Blue Buck Shoal on the Sabine was the most notorious, though the Indian Creek Shoal on the Angelina presented as many problems. Riverbank trees sometimes hung so far out over the water as to be a hazard, as were steep bluffs which dropped crashing into the water now and then, and sometimes upon the river vessel. For many reasons, then, rivermen preferred to travel at high water times. There was less chance of disaster, and the current moved faster.

Generally speaking, our Texas river people were rivermen on a part-time basis. Very often they were farmers who wished to supplement their incomes with the cash a river trip might bring. Farmers had usually borrowed heavily on their crops even before they were harvested, and could expect to take home no cash, or at least very little. Part of the farmers' cash went to the riverman who shipped his crop downriver. This cash the riverman might invest in a farm of his own — slaves, tools, or, as seems to have been the case several times, partial payment for machinery for a cotton gin — wherein he could get even more of the farmers' cash in the coming year. Taking a hypothetical situation, we might consider a poor boy who had served in the Revolutionary Army and had gotten a grant of land. He, and maybe his wife and a little child comprised his household. Working his fingers to the bone, he and his wife might clear a fifteen or twenty acre field and plant cotton and corn. For seed and equipment he necessarily went into debt at the local store, and when he made his crop, his profit was applied to the debt. The next planting time he might plant more land, cleared in the cold months; but he would still have to borrow. He envisioned having slaves, but to buy a slave he needed cash, or at least a partial payment. To get that cash, since he has, remember, absolutely nothing but his land and bare essentials with which to farm, he can, very inexpensively, become a riverman. From trees on his land (trees which he has to get rid of anyway) he fashions a raft or maybe even a flatboat, if he has the energy to split the logs. At never less than one dollar a bale and sometimes three dollars, he will agree to ship his neighbors' cotton to the coast, or to some downriver center. In doing so, he eliminates the cost of shipping his own bales, and reaps a percent of each bale his clients have made. Hiring a local youth or two, he puts his plain vessel into the river current, and by means of long poles and a watchful eye, guides it to his destination. At the market he places the cotton with the various business houses with which the upcounty farmers have dealt through traveling agents or by mail. What money is involved he secures in a moneybelt (if the farmer has not arranged to have it deposited at a coastal bank), and walks home, or perhaps buys a horse and rides, or catches a keelboat, traveling free, in exchange for his services as a deck hand. Back home he finds himself with cash payment from the farmers, cash payment for the vessel he sold to a lumber dealer, and cash from his crop, which he applies to his debt. The extra money, then, he may use to expand his farm — maybe the down-payment on a slave, maybe another money-making device. The hard labor of river life he takes for granted in his quest for success, doubtless when he has acquired slaves and is therefore able to have a large, highly profitable farm, he will retire from the river and settle to being a **planter** — thus fulfilling the ideal that has brought him to this wilderness woods.

  The story is rather typical. Full time rivermen had difficulty in building a reputation strong enough to warrant farmers to entrust valuable cotton to them. The most esteemed asset of a riverman was his honesty and dependability. As a local farmer himself, he was more likely to get clients, because the planters knew he would return to his interests upriver — and would not do as some, take off to Mexico or the United States with the money. Some of these youthful entrepreneurs became so fond of the river life and found it so much more exciting and profitable than farming, that they remained on the rivers, keeping "model farms" and developing a career as rivermen. It is many of these men who were later to be the captains of steamboats, purchased through investors, or through an accumulation of saved cash.

The most usual means of traveling the rivers was the raft. This was nothing more than a series of logs bound together. The bales and bundles were secured to the flat surface with ropes and covered by various means — economical tree bark, or the more desirable canvas.

Superior to the raft was the flatboat, which was essentially flat surface with sides and a roof of timbers. Ordinarily the wood was hewn, squared off, and left rough; the roof was of long members which were water bent and made an excellent shelter from the elements.[3] Beneath the roof was principally a freight area, but also a tiny cabin with a hearth for a fire, the smoke of which escaped through a hole in the roof. Squarenosed and boxlike, the flatboat was kept in the current and off the riverbank by long, tough poles, which, like giant toothpicks, served to push the boat away from dangerous obstructions. For flatboats there was no turning back and there was no stopping, except by a gentle guiding into a marsh, a sandbar, a riverbank, or by throwing a rope to someone on the shore who could immediately fix the rope to a tree as anchor.[4] The flatboat never made the return trip upriver, but was sold, for sometimes as high as thirty dollars, for the lumber it contained. A boat fifty feet long by fifteen feet wide could be employed in building a house, if for nothing else than the strong framing timbers. Old Sabine Pass and present-day Galveston had houses built of flatboats, and I know at least one upcountry house which shows the traces of nautical ancestry, but whether it is a flatboat or keelboat, I do not know.

The keelboat was a more sophisticated proposition than a flatboat. It was built to last. The best keelboat description I've ever heard was that it was like a "little Noah's Ark." Truly the keelboat resembled an ark with its fat, bulbous sides and its rounded, pointing ends. It had a full cabin with windows (not glass, of course), and a ponderous freight section. Its roof was of the same bent timbers as had the flatboats. There was a huge, removable rudder, which could be attached at either end. While poles were still used at troublesome times, the rudder solved myriad problems, particularly that of keeping the boat in the current.[5] The downriver journey of the keelboat was virtually the same as the flatboat, only simpler. Where three men were a minimum crew for a flatboat, two men could operate the keelboat on its downriver trip. The upriver passage, however, was an adventure within itself. Crews were not hard to obtain — usually the flatboatmen wanted the job for free passage home. The keelboat was emptied of upcountry cotton, corn, and tobacco, and filled with store-bought goods. Ordinarily the riverman's farmer clients had given him lists of merchandise he could obtain for them and subtract the price from the cotton money, or attach it to their account at this or that business house. Filling the keelboat full of things — calico, iron parlor stoves, plows, saddles, tin bathtubs — the arduous return began. Human power replaced that of the rivercurrent. By poling or by towing, the riverman and his crew of a minimum four, and preferably six, inched the boat back home. Poling involved using the long, strong poles and pushing the boat with them by standing at certain spots on the deck and fixing the poles against the riverbottom. A man on the shore kept a rope taut between the boat and a tree, so as not to lose any of the laborous advance. When towing was possible, the riverbank being treeless, the crew pulled the vessel by means of long ropes. The keelboat was kept as far into the fringes of the current as safety would allow; near the shore were calmer waters, hence less strain from the opposing thrust of the river. At best the work was incomparably hard and involved constant attention, except when the boat was tied up for the night.

One faulty move, the drop of a rope, the break of a pole, and the entire keelboat and crew could saunter into current and began falling downriver wildly in disarray.

It was perhaps in the keelboat that the Texas riverman first identified himself. A keelboat man was referred to as "captain" and he willingly assumed the role and dressed the part; he invariably named his vessel the **Jasper,** the **Ship of State,** the **Rosaltha,** the **Rock and Rye** — and he was proud of her. Sometimes he painted her — blue, red, yellow, or white, and if he was very ingenious he usually experimented with attaching a great sail to her. The sails did not work on the narrow Texas rivers, it seems to be universally recorded.

Steamboats did not end the era of the flatboat and the keelboat, but they permanently thinned out those vessels, which had dominated the rivers throughout the 1830s. Steamboating added an aura of sophistication to the upcountry woods which had not been there before. Now it was possible to travel to Galveston in comfort, if not great style; it was possible to almost eliminate the risk of losing cotton in overturns and breakups, by shipping aboard the fine riverboats. Rivermen became businessmen, and made money in quantities they had not previously believed possible. Coastal products became available to the backwoodsmen, as were imports, shipped to Galveston aboard one of many schooners — the **Eclipse,** the **American Trader,** the **Waterwitch,** the **Only Son.**[6] From Galveston the goods could safely travel the Sabine, the Trinity, the Brazos, the Neches, to the upland cabins, unharmed and with minimal danger. It was worth even the heavy tariffs of the Republic of Texas to have luxuries which one had not seen in a decade.

The first steamer whistle heard in the piney woods was at Gaines Ferry in 1837. Captains Wright and Delmore took their **Velocipede** a hundred twenty-five-foot steamboat, up the Sabine in a pioneering and money-making venture. By May of 1839, steamboats plied the Sabine regularly. On New Year's Day, 1840 the **Rufus Putnam** left Galveston Island for Gaines Ferry under the sponsorship of J. Temple Doswell, Esquire, who announced that "parties desiring to attend the sale of lots at Sabine City" could depend upon the boat leaving at the appointed time."[7]

The **Yellowstone** penetrated the Brazos backwaters as early as 1834 and steamed as far inland as Washington-on-the-Brazos. It was reserved purely for high water, however, as at least one steamer found herself stranded for many months because of the dropping water level. The **Laura** also appeared on the Brazos in the early 1830s; this famous steamer was the first to climb Buffalo Bayou as far as the city of Houston, and her trip was performed not long after the Battle of San Jacinto.[8]

The town of Liberty was for years the highest connection available on the plantation-banked Trinity. Liberty was sixty-six miles by water from the Gulf and one hundred forty-three miles from Galveston Island. Five hundred bales was considered a rather average cargo on the Trinity, and the cargoes sometimes rose to fifteen hundred bales aboard one boat. By the same token, five thousand barrels is a maximum recorded cargo on that river — the freight was one dollar and a half per wet barrel and one dollar per dry barrel.[9] In 1839 **Correo** traveled to the town of Carolina, two hundred miles up the Trinity from the Gulf; in the next year the steamer **Trinity** made a record five hundred mile trip to the hamlet of Alabama.[10] Regular passage those long distances varied as years went by, according to the demand.

Of the Colorado River we know very little, except that it was not desirable for steamboat travel. In 1840 the **Swan** was at Matagorda claiming to have journeyed up the Colorado to LaGrange — we don't know whether she did or not. We do know that the **Betty Powell** was built at LaGrange in 1853 from riverbottom timbers. A great barbecue was held and "dinner on the ground" to celebrate the launching of the **Betty Powell**. She was launched in the grandest country style, but proved too big for the river, and never again saw the fair fields of LaGrange, but was used on other rivers for twenty-five years.[11]

The Neches River was a late arrival to the river trade, where steamboats were concerned. The Neches and the Angelina were ideally suited for flatboats and keelboats, causing no pressing demand for steamers. So it was not until 1848 that the first steamboat arrived at Bevilport, the principal riverport of Jasper County, where the Angelina poured into the Neches, two hundred forty miles by river from the Gulf of Mexico. Throughout the 1850s the **Sunflower** claimed most of the Neches trade. She was followed in 1866 by the **Camargo**, and finally the **Laura**, whose brilliant career was ended in the 1890s by log jams in the river. This **Laura** is not to be confused with the one previously described. The **Laura** had a well-documented life, and we might consider her typical of the riverboats, which changed very little from the eighteen thirties to the eighteen seventies, in which decade they began their decline. On the Mississippi the **Laura** would not have been considered anything mentionable; for a Texas river, her credentials were different. She was one hundred fifteen feet long, thirty-two feet of beam. Her two levels of decks were well-made, glowing under a coat of white paint. On the upper deck were lines of green louvered doors which led to the passenger cabins and the saloon. She was a sternwheeler, and on each side in flowery letters was painted her name. The cabins are described as "tiny and well made with mahogany and brass fittings." In the saloon were upholstered armchairs, sofas, a cumbersome Empire sideboard, pictures, mirrors, a square-grand piano, and a long cloth-covered table with chairs pulled up to it. An uncovered staircase led from the second deck to the first level, where there was a huge storage area for freight. She was primarily a freight boat, with capacity of six hundred bales, and without the cotton, seventeen hundred barrels, and "several hundred" boxes. She could make the trip from her home port of Bevilport to the destination of Sabine Pass in twenty-two days. The mate made forty dollars per month; the deckhands averaged twenty-five dollars per month. She was owned by a corporation of five investors.[12]

Steamboat captains were rarely part-time rivermen, for the incomes from steamers were so large and so varied that the boats were taken downriver as often as possible. Contracts for shipping to backwoods storekeepers brought substantial profits, in addition to shipping for individual farmers and the money made from passenger fares. In Galveston, the mecca for the rivermen, captains met at their favorite haunts — Francois' Hotel, built in a wrecked ship and advertising a "French Criolla" cook: the Warsaw Hotel, with its celebrated baths; the Tremont House with its legendary cocktails; and for the wilder side of life, the Monroe Edwards Saloon, Hotel, and Dance Hall, which specialized in "Sailors, Adventurers, and Sharps." In the company of schooner masters and the captains of great Gulf boats like the **New York** and the **Lafitte**, backwoods steamer captains made advantageous deals on purchasing goods and shipping their clients' cotton at special rates to New Orleans, Boston, New York, the West Indies, and Liverpool.[13]

While the flatboatman and the keelboatman sometimes retired to rural dignity, the steamboat captain was rarely satisfied with the placid life on the land, the Farmer's Almanac, and cotton growing in the fields. He grew accustomed to having money in his pocket and he liked to stay out of debt, unless he found a good buy on a steamboat. Steamboats became his life. A Jasper County riverman jeopardized his hard-earned security of a farm to make the big splash and buy an eleven thousand dollar steamboat. That was the **Laura**. The Kennedy Brothers risked a fortune to prove a point in taking their **Lost Heir** on an eight month, eight hundred ninety-three mile trip to Dallas from Galveston. They arrived in May of 1868, and their only satisfaction was to have opened the Trinity River's upper reaches to navigation.

The riverman's world came to an end not with crescendo, but slowly and indefinitely. Railroads, to begin with, lessened the demand for riverboats, and this became more evident as the nineteenth century wore into its last decades. Log jams became an obstruction which in some cases blocked the rivers for as much as three months at a time, imprisoning the riverboats at up-country landings, or serving as a barrier to keep them from returning home. In comparison to the railroads, riverboats were slow and not as safe; in convenience, the vessels did not compete. The log jams of the 1880s merely completed the picture. Surrendering, some rivermen turned to the sawmills for careers, others went to the land and planted, retaining only the title "captain" to associate them with the past. As the times changed, so the emphasis upon waterways changed, and the little river-stops rotted away, losing population and life to cities on railroads and highways.

The river people's world today clings to abandoned, weed-choked waterfronts and manuscripts stuffed into forgotten places. Because their physical traces are so sparse — at best, it is difficult to sense the riverman's place in nineteenth century Texas.

Notes

1. Andrew F. Smyth to Geo. W. Smyth, Esq., Moulton, Alabama, April 14, 1835. Cited in William Seale, **Texas Riverman: The Life and Times of Captain Andrew Smyth** (Austin, 1966).

2. A sampling of materials on this may be found in **Ashbel Smith MS.**, University of Texas Archives; **George W. Smyth MS.**, University of Texas Archives; **John Salmon Ford MS.**, University of Texas Archives; **Gail Borden's Customshouse Notebook**, Rosenberg Library, Galveston; **George Marshall MS.**, Duke University Library; Max Freund (ed.), **Gustav Dresel's Houston Journal** (Austin, 1954); Eugene Hollon and Ruth L. Butler (eds.), **William Bollaert's Texas** (Norman, 1956).

3. Flatboat notes of Capt. Andrew Smyth, dated Bevilport and Walnut Run Plantation, Texas, 1843-1850, cited in **Texas Riverman**.

4. Ibid., notes on an improvement survey of the Neches and Angelina rivers (up to Indian Creek Shoal), dated 1859 and 1875; Ibid., newspaper clipping dealing with river obstructions, obviously a 19th century newspaper, but undated; **Ben Stuart MS.**, Rosenberg Library, Galveston, Texas.

5. The classic keelboat is described and pictured in Leland D. Baldwin's **The Keelboat Age on Western Waters** (Pittsburgh, 1941), certainly the most authoritative account published to date. A simple drawing in Captain Andrew Smyth's papers indicates great similarity between the boats Baldwin describes and illustrates and those used in Texas, the latter ones being perhaps more narrow. The Smyth diagram is undated, and is in his unpublished manuscripts.

6. Ben Stuart MS.
7. Ibid.
8. An account of both vessels is found in William R. Hogan, The Texas Republic, (Norman, 1946).
9. Ben Stuart MS.
10. Ibid.
11. Ibid.
12. Seale, Texas Riverman, 144-159.
13. Ben Stuart MS.; Day Book of Doctor Dyer, MS., Rosenberg Library, Galveston, Texas.

6

East Texas in the Election of 1860 and the Secession Crisis

by
Allan C. Ashcraft

Allan C. Ashcraft is a Professor of History at Texas A&M University, and a Past President of the East Texas Historical Association. He is the author of **Texas in the Civil War**, and numerous related articles.

6

In 1860, the State of Texas was reputed to be a land of opportunity and was experiencing rapid settlement. The past decade had seen the population increase three-fold. There were now 151 counties that stretched along the entire Rio Grande boundary and, elsewhere, covered the state as far as the 100th meridian (the line that marks the eastern limit of the Panhandle). Within this organized area there were several distinctive agricultural regions: the eastern and southeastern part of the state was characterized by extensive cotton production; the central and northern portion was the site of diversified agriculture; while the western and southwestern section had a combination of subsistence food crops and stock raising.[1]

Texas was most heavily settled in the eastern and southeastern area, where a number of cotton plantations had been established. Several factors worked to restrict extensive cotton production to this zone. First of all was the matter of soil fertility. Early agriculturalists maintained that high fertility was indicated by heavy stands of native hard wood timber. Because of this, prospective planters invested much time and labor in killing heavy underbrush, and in girdling and burning trees so as to clear these timbered tracts for planting. Relatively clean land was avoided; it was "obviously infertile," and its hard packed prairie type soil was frequently too difficult for the crude, early plows to break.[2]

A second limiting factor to large scale cotton planting was rainfall. This was of special importance in the latter years of the 1850s because Texas was suffering from a drought cycle. Even the very optimistic **Texas Almanac** of 1861 reluctantly had to admit that the 97 degree line (running almost through Dallas) had now come to mark the start of the drought hazard region. A final key factor that limited the great cotton plantation area involved transportation considerations. Because of a serious lack of adequate railway facilities, and because of the prohibitive costs of overland ox-cart hauling, cotton producers wisely chose to locate their lands on the lower navigable limits of the Texas river systems.[3]

Mainly because of these reasons, the ideal plantations were developed in the river valleys of the state: the Guadalupe, the Colorado, the Brazos, the Trinity, the Neches, the Sabine, and the Red. But even within these individual valleys there were further limiting factors. For example, coastal marsh lands were prominent near the mouths of rivers that emptied into the Gulf in the southeastern corner of the state. These lands obviously had to be avoided. And, even in the fertile heartland of some of the valleys, navigational peculiarities of the rivers caused local transportation difficulties that discouraged planters from locating there. Such was the case in the lower Trinity River valley. It was noted that rains along the lower Trinity would mostly flow off to raise the neighboring San Jacinto and Neches rivers. In order for the Trinity to reach a safe depth for steamboats, heavy rains far upstate were required. Such rains were not too dependable, causing much concern for the farmers and steamboat captains involved.[4] After all, an absence of adequate rainfall in the upper Trinity basin could well force an overland marketing of the cotton. At standard freight rates of 20¢ per ton mile, a trip of 100 miles would absorb the profits of 11¢ cotton.[5]

While the term "East Texas" today refers to a way of life as much as a geographical region, several learned publications have bravely offered a rough boundary line for "East Texas." According to the **Handbook of Texas**, this dividing line runs along a lazy arc from Red River County (on the Oklahoma border) through Leon County, and then on down to Galveston Bay.[6] Based on the 1860 development of Texas, this zone included at least 36 counties, and extended sufficiently far west to include major portions of: Red River, Titus, Wood, Smith, Anderson, Leon, Madison, Grimes, Montgomery, Harris and Galveston counties. In terms of population, these counties included over 34% of the white population of Texas, while over 43% of the slaves resided there.[7]

Based on 1860 census reports, these East Texas counties varied widely in agricultural and economic success. Counties considered "poor" in cotton production and almost completely lacking in plantation development were: Chambers, Galveston, Hardin, Harris, Jefferson, Orange, Madison, and Wood. Of these, all but the last two consisted of coastal marsh lands. As for Madison and Wood counties, they were both located in such positions as to have no ready access to dependable river transportation. In these eight "poor" cotton counties there were but 51 holders of over 20 slaves and only two farms of over 500 acres in size.

On the other hand, "rich" East Texas cotton counties included: Walker, Polk, Montgomery, Harrison, Bowie, and Grimes. Each of these had immediate or short land haul access to navigable streams. While only a half dozen in number, these counties contained over ⅓ of the sizable slave holdings in East Texas, and this same county group had over 40% of the land holdings above 500 acres to be found in East Texas. Nearly ⅓ of East Texas' vast cotton crop was produced in these six very rich counties.

The remaining counties ranged widely between these two great agricultural extremes. Some, such as San

Augustine, Rusk, and Cass counties included an impressive number of plantations. Others, such as Angelina, Nacogdoches, and Trinity counties had very few planters in their impressive populations of yeomen farmers.

Although faint signs of a political cleavage between East Texas and the western part of the state came to light in the middle 1850s,[8] by the latter part of the decade these intra-state points of controversy had become far overshadowed by national problems that were shaking the Union to its very foundation. Consistent outspoken critic of extreme sectional views was Sam Houston. In 1857, the old hero, while still serving his final two years as United States Senator, was defeated in his race for governor of Texas. In 1859, however, Houston managed to capitalize on a lull in extremist feelings and to win the gubernatorial election of that year. Later in 1859, the short period of relative sectional calm came to an abrupt termination with John Brown's raid. Inflamed Southern tempers hit the boiling point. In Texas, this was clearly indicated on the political scene in December, when the enraged legislature selected Louis T. Wigfall to fill a vacancy in the United States Senate. Wigfall, a resident of Marshall since 1848, was the greatest Southern extremist in the state and had long been a blood political enemy of Sam Houston. His elevation was an obvious and blatant affront to the governor and to Unionism.

Brown's raid caused Southern sensitivities to burn with emotionalism. Throughout the South there were protest mass meetings and wholesale denunciations of his "abolitionist scheme." This was true, also, in East Texas, where, for example, a meeting of citizens was held at Palestine (Anderson County) in late December. The townspeople roundly damned the "covert, dark, unholy, and fanatical" plot of abolitionists to infiltrate the South in the guise of peddlers and teachers. A board was established to seize and publicly to burn all dangerous books. Vigilance committees were authorized to seek out abolitionist spies. The town merchants were enjoined to cease all purchases from anti-slavery business houses of the North. In addition, teachers of

Northern birth were only to be hired when "by long residence among us we know their soundness." Finally, there was to be a suppression of all music adjudged to be "dangerous to and subversive of the Constitutional rights and liberties of the South!"⁹

Events of 1860 brought even more vividly to East Texas imaginations the horrors to be expected from abolitionist inspired slave revolts. That summer saw a number of very destructive fires break out in northeastern Texas. Towns such as Henderson, Dallas, Denton, Waxahachie, and Jefferson reported either actual fires or confirmed attempts at incendiary actions. While conservative elements in the state denied that the fires had taken place or else claimed them to have been accidental, the **Texas Republican** newspaper of Marshall revealed the East Texas reaction to the fire reports:

> Whatever exaggerations there may have been in the recent incendiary movements (and we admit there have been many exaggerations) in Texas, one thing is evident, they have been too numerous to have resulted from accident. Over a million of dollars worth of property has been destroyed in the course of a few weeks. And if we are to place any reliance in the testimony elicited by an examination of the negroes, all these outrages were the work of abolition emissaries.¹⁰

Citizens of Carthage (Panola County) were typical of worried East Texans when they held a mass meeting and petitioned the County Court to set up a county-wide patrol system, to search all Negro quarters for weapons, to guard slaves closely and to keep them away from towns, to clear all wooded town lots that might conceal troublemakers, to punish groups of three or more slaves away from home (even if they had passes), and to organize defensive volunteer militia forces.¹¹

In Jacksonville (Cherokee County), the resurrected patrol system was reinforced with an all-night alert of white men on the night of a rumored attempt at slave revolt.¹²

The neighboring states of Arkansas and Louisiana expressed grave concern over near revolts and real fires reported in northeastern Texas. The Van Buren **Press** carried the glaring warning: "Fearful Abolition Raid — Insurrection of Negroes — Ossawotamee Brown Among Us — Northern Texas to be Laid Waste — the Work Already Commenced."[13] While the sturdy New Orleans **Picayune** solemnly advised its readers not to purchase slaves from the "tainted districts" of Texas where fires and near rebellions proved that the Negroes had been "tampered with."[14]

With events thus set, the election of 1860 drew near. Texas delegates to the Democratic Convention at Charleston, South Carolina, walked out with the lower South and subsequently supported the candidacy of Breckinridge as standard bearer for the Southern Democrats. At Chicago, citizens of the Lone Star State were highly incensed to learn that eight Texas delegates had presented themselves before the Republican Convention. So unsympathetic was Texas with the Republican Party that a movement was started among Texas newspapers to publicize the names and to prepare fitting punishments for these eight "abolitionist dastards who dared to misrepresent this State, in the Black Republican convention."[15] Elsewhere, in Baltimore, two Texans represented the state at the Constitutional Union Convention. One of these Texans was a rather hairy character named Colonel A. B. Norton, who had sworn twelve years earlier neither to shave nor to cut his hair until Henry Clay was elected President of the United States. Both Norton and his Texas associate pushed for the nomination of Sam Houston by this conservative, almost pitiful group. On the second ballot, however, John Bell of Tennessee was given the nomination.

Finally, amidst threats and boasts of secession, amidst burning editorials that sought to invoke the words of American immortals to support all sides of the arguments at hand, amidst deep fears over the safety of property and lives, the people of Texas made their ways to the polls. Texas ballots offered but two choices of names in the election — Breckinridge, candidate of the strong Southern rights faction that was now recognized as the Southern Democrats, and Bell, conservative candidate of the Constitutional Union Party.

In over-all voting figures, East Texas showed a slight above-the-average participation in the election. Support for Bell (22.4% of East Texas votes) was a little below the state average of 24.4% for the Constitutional Unionist candidate. No East Texas county gave Bell a majority. However, he carried between 1/4 and 1/3 of the vote in 13 counties. These counties fall into four categories on the basis of their agricultural productivity. "Poor" farm counties offering significant support for Bell were: Galveston, Harris, and Wood. But, commercial interests in both Galveston and Harris counties doubtlessly had quite an influence on the voting. Wood County, "poor" in agriculture and with no commerce at stake, defies explanation for its minority support of Bell. Similarly, there is no ready explanation for the two small farmer counties of Angelina and Nacogdoches, both of which offered strong minority favor for Bell. The remaining counties were either the "rich" planter counties of Bowie, Grimes, Harrison, and Montgomery, or the large farmer counties of Marion, Red River, Cass, and Rusk. The fact that these counties showed an interest in Bell suggests a feeling of conservatism among those with well-established plantations and large farms. These individuals had large slave holdings, were producing considerable numbers of profitable bales, and, in some cases, were of the old conservative Whig tradition.[16]

In all of East Texas there were but four counties that offered Bell over 1/3 of their votes. These were: Angelina and Nacogdoches, small farmer counties; Red River, a large farmer county; and Harrison, a planter county. Obviously, no trend is evident here.

When the national election results were made known and Lincoln and the "Black Republicans" were declared winners, a powerful reaction was seen throughout the South. State flags replaced the national ensign, mass meetings were again held, and the name of Lincoln was uttered like a curse. East Texas reaction was typified by Marshall (Harrison County):

> The excitement in Marshall, upon the news of Lincoln's election, has never been surpassed if equalled,

103

within the brief history of the Lone Star State. Judging from our exchanges, the people were not more temperate in other localities of this, & other Southern States. . . . A pole was in readiness upon the reception of the news, at the top of which to hoist the Lone Star flag. The sad intelligence as anticipated came, and up went the Star, followed by shouts, firing of cannon and the uptossing of hats, old and new.[17]

This outburst was followed by a series of speeches in which one citizen, Gil McKay declared: "Yes, fellow-citizens of Texas, I can't say as I once could, fellow-citizens of the United States. I say it in sorrow, but I am no longer a citizen of the United States."[18]

The Cherokee County courthouse was topped with a Texas flag, while an effigy of Lincoln hung on the northwest corner of the courthouse square.[19]

A Harrison County mass meeting indicted the North for such offenses as breaking the Constitution by ignoring the Fugitive Slave law, limiting slave holding rights in territories, packing the Supreme Court to secure a reversal of the Dred Scott decision, eventually wanting to end slavery, encouraging slave revolts, electing a sectional president, and charging that the South had no right to secede. Because of these manifold crimes, the meeting went on record as preferring:

> . . . restoration to that independence for which she [Texas] once enjoyed, to the ignomy ensuing from sectional dictation, sorrowing for the mistake she has committed in sacrificing her independence at the alter of her patriotism, she should unfurl again the banner of the "Lone Star" to the breeze and re-enter upon a national career, where if no glory awaits her, she will at least be free from a subjection, by might, to wrong and shame.[20]

Finally, to add to the Texans' confusion, fear, and insecurity, East Texas suddenly became a prime recruiting grounds for the Knights of the Golden Circle. "General" George W. L. Bickley spent the last two months of 1860 there enrolling young men in his movement. As popularly advertised, the order stood as a Southern counterpart to the "Wide Awakes," a Republican young men's auxiliary that was denounced as a militaristic command formed "to enforce Black Republican misrule upon the South."[21]

By December, because of Sam Houston's refusal to follow the example of the lower Southern states in calling for a Secession Convention, four leading Texas citizens issued a call for voters to select delegates to a state Secession Convention that was called to order in late January. On February 1, the body approved an Ordinance of Secession and asked for the people of Texas to ratify the adoption of the document by a general election to be held on February 23. Meanwhile, before the voice of the people could be heard, the Convention's watchdog Committee of Public Safety secured the surrender of Federal military posts in the state and made arrangements for the evacuation of United States soldiers normally assigned to the District of Texas. It was also during this interim period that the Convention's delegation arrived in Montgomery, Alabama, to represent Texas in the forming of the Provisional Confederate Government.

As the day for the popular vote on secession drew near, the newspapers of Texas did what they could to shape opinions. While a very few sheets asked for cool heads and second thinking on the folly of disunion and possible rebellion, the great bulk of editors pointed out the advantages of independence and called on Texas to meet its responsibility in giving the lower South a solid front in the secession movement. Typical of East Texas press appeals in favor of the Ordinance was that of the Marshall **Texas Republican**:

> The Constitution of our country . . . has been trampled in the dust. The federative system inaugurated by it . . . is destroyed! An abolition President is about to be inaugurated — a man who is surrounded by the advocates of John Brown, the endorsers of Helper, the proclaimers of the "irrepressible conflict" and the equality of the races. He and his party are pledged to our subjugation, and threatens us with the sword if we dare to resist.[22]

As for the grim prophecy that disunion would be followed by war, the average newspaper cast severe doubt on this possibility. One editor explained:

> But we have never believed, and do not yet, that war can or will take place. If the Black Republicans provoke it, they will soon find their mistake, and from being the invaders, their country will be entered triumphantly by a Southern army.[23]

Other Texas editors took the threat of war so lightly that they playfully repeated lampooning reports from papers of the lower South:

> Charleston, Supper-time, Jan. 15 — All babies in the entire South are in arms, and many in the city are now employed at the breast-works.[24]

In late February, the popular referendum on the Secession Ordinance took place. The Convention then reassembled in early March, canvassed the votes, and announced that secession had been carried by a majority of three to one.

East Texans, like their fellow citizens throughout the state, cast considerably fewer ballots in this election than they had cast in the recent presidential contest. The counties of the east staunchly supported secession with an overwhelming vote of almost nine to one. Only Angelina County in all of East Texas voted against secession. Angelina had likewise given Bell a strong minority vote in the earlier election. Eleven counties voted over 10% against secession. These were the "poor" agricultural counties of Hardin, Harris, and Wood: the small farmer counties of Angelina, Nacogdoches, Sabine; and Titus; the large farmer county of Leon; and the "rich" planter counties of Montgomery and Walker. Six of these counties had given Bell significant support in 1860.[25]

Five East Texas counties were sufficiently cool towards secession to offer over 25% of their votes against it. Of these five, only Red River and Titus had farms over 500 acres (15 in all), and only they had substantial holdings of over 20 slaves. In all of the five counties there were but 73 slave holders. Hardin and Wood counties were "poor" agricultural areas with no indication of plantation development. Small farmer Angelina County was consistently a rebel that defies explanation.

The bulk of these "cool toward secession" counties formed a block in northeastern Texas. This was one of the few parts of Texas inhabited by individuals of Northern backgrounds and with Northern ties.[26] As war developed, many of these persons packed their wagons and headed out of the state. One traveler, journeying through this part of Texas, noted that in a one-day period he passed an estimated 500 wagons that were moving northward across the state boundary.[27]

Thus the record stands. Noticeable trends for East Texas were these:
1. In the election of 1860 there was a slight favoring for the conservative candidate Bell in several planter and large farmer counties. However, the over-all trend for East Texas was quite representative of the whole state's voting pattern in this election.
2. In the secession election, East Texas showed an overwhelming unanimity for secession. While the state favored disunion by a three to one vote, East Texas supported it almost nine to one. East Texas counties least enthusiastic towards secession were generally "poor" or small farmer, and were mostly located in a block in the northern part of the sector.
3. East Texas' strong stand in favor of secession was also reflected by its very powerful support of the Southern Cause during the resulting Civil War. East Texas provided a tremendous number of volunteer regiments for the South. East Texas exhibited none of the organized pockets of disloyalty to be found in western and southwestern Texas. East Texas was the site of the most notable prisoner of war camps in the state (Camp Ford and Camp Groce). East Texas was the location of several depots and headquarters installations for the Department of the Trans-Mississippi West (such as a financial and repair center near Marshall and a beef packing plant at Jefferson). East Texas provided Kirby Smith's unofficial alternate headquarters at

Marshall. East Texas furnished a seat for the Missouri Confederate capital in exile. East Texas was the scene of the Confederacy's most spectacular small-scale victory (at Sabine Pass). In short, East Texas took a strong stand on secession and then willingly did its utmost to meet the bloody consequences to follow.

Notes

1. Agricultural regions have been plotted on the basis of 1860 census information. **Agriculture of the United States in 1860; Compiled from the Original Returns of the Eighth Census** (Washington, 1884), 140-49.
2. Frederick Law Olmsted, **A Journey to Texas** (New York, 1857). Captain Flack, **The Texan Rifle-Hunter** (London, 1857), 61-62.
3. **Texas Almanac — 1861** (Galveston, 1860), 189.
4. Ibid., 122-26.
5. Charles W. Ramsdell, "Internal Improvements Projects in Texas in the 1850's" in **Proceedings of the Mississippi Valley Historical Association**, IX, pt. 1., 99-100.
6. **The Handbook of Texas** (Austin, 1952), I, 534-35.
7. Figures taken from **Population of the United States in 1860; Compiled from Original Returns of the Eighth Census** (Washington, 1864).
8. Charles W. Ramsdell, "The Frontier and Secession" in **Studies in Southern History and Politics Subscribed to William Archibald Dunning** (New York, 1914).
9. Trinity Advocate (Palestine), Jan. 4, 1860 in Ollinger Crenshaw, **The Slave States in the Presidential Election of 1860** (Baltimore, 1945), 90.
10. Texas Republican (Marshall), Sept. 8, 1860.
11. Ibid., Aug. 18, 1860.
12. Hattie J. Roach, **A History of Cherokee County** (Dallas, 1934), 61.
13. David Y. Thomas, **Arkansas in War and Reconstruction 1861-1874** (Little Rock, 1926), 23.
14. Evening Picayune (New Orleans), Aug. 18, 1860 in William W. White, "The Texas Slave Insurrection of 1860" in **The Southwestern Historical Quarterly**, LII, No. 3, Jan. 1949, 279-80.
15. The Seguin Mercury, May 30, 1860.
16. Figures taken from W. Dean Burnham, **Presidential Ballots 1836-1892** (Baltimore, 1955), 764-812.
17. The Harrison Flag (Marshall), Nov. 24, 1860.
18. Ibid.

19. Roach, Cherokee County, 61.
20. Texan Republican (Marshall), Dec. 1, 1860.
21. Ibid., Nov. 17, 1860. Jimmie Hicks, "Some Letters Concerning the Knights of the Golden Circle in Texas, 1860-1861" in The Southwestern Historical Quarterly, LXV, No. 1, July, 1961, 81.
22. Texas Republican (Marshall), Feb. 23, 1861.
23. Ibid., March 2, 1861.
24. The Southern Confederacy (Seguin), March 8, 1861.
25. Figures taken from Executive Record Book, No. 279, 222-23. Texas State Archives.
26. Charles W. Ramsdell, **Reconstruction in Texas** (New York: Columbia University, 1910), 11-12.
27. Annie H. Abel, **Indians as Secessionists** (Cleveland, 1915), 95. The Southern Confederacy, June 7, 1861.

7

Life in Civil War East Texas

by
Ralph A. Wooster

Ralph A. Wooster is Regents Professor of History and Dean of the Graduate School at Lamar University. He is a past President of the East Texas Historical Association, the Texas State Historical Association, and of the Texas Association of College Teachers. He is the author of **The Secession Conventions of the South, The People in Power,** and **Planters and Plain Folk** as well as some 40 articles.

7

On March 2, 1861, exactly twenty-five years after Texas declared her independence from Mexico, the secession convention meeting in Austin announced that the voters of the state had overwhelmingly approved an ordinance of separation and that Texas was no longer a member of the union of American states. Quickly the convention moved to formalize the vote of the people to pass an ordinance uniting Texas with the newly formed Confederate States of America.[1] This action marked the beginning of a four year struggle by the people of Texas and her sister Southern states to establish an independent Southern nation extending from the Atlantic on the east to the Rio Grande on the west.

The work of the secession convention was warmly applauded throughout most of the state. In some areas, especially in the north central counties of the Red River country and in the German settlements of central Texas, there were misgivings, and a few state leaders, notably Governor Sam Houston, refused to recognize the new

Confederate government, but on the whole secession was popular with the people of Texas. In the eastern portion of the state, scene of the rich cotton lands, coastal prairies, and rustling timbers as well as the urban port of Galveston and its new, growing inland rival Houston, the withdrawal was an occasion for rejoicing. Only one East Texas county, Angelina, cast a majority of her votes in the popular referendum against secession and much of the impetus for secession had come from East Texas political leaders such as Hardin R. Runnels, O. M. Roberts, and T. Jefferson Chambers.[2] In most towns of East Texas militia units paraded noisily, cannon boomed and flags were waved by the enthusiastic citizenry. In Galveston, commercial outlet for the cotton trade, British consul Arthur Lynn noted that the atmosphere was "one of joy and congratulation that they can now free themselves from a connection which had been injurious to their interests."[3] Everywhere there was a spirit of enthusiasm, excitement, and optimism that the war would be short and that the South would at last be free from Northern oppression.[4]

In the next few weeks there were scenes throughout the state of recruiting, enlisting, and drilling new troops. In many towns whole companies were mustered in at once as were the W. P. Lane Rangers, who were sworn in at a public ceremony witnessed by hundreds of enthusiastic townspeople in Marshall.[5] Others enlisted singly as did Beaumonter William A. Fletcher, who was so eager to volunteer that he rushed immediately to Houston to offer his services:

> I was on the roof of a two-story house putting on the finishing course of shingles [Fletcher wrote in his memoirs] when Captain William Rogers came by and reported war declared and the fall of Fort Sumter. The news was brought from Sabine Pass by an up-river steamer that had just landed, and it made me very nervous thinking of the delay of completing the roof might cause me to miss a chance to enlist, so I worked and talked and soon had the roof finished, and made an arrangement with Rogers that I would take the train the next day for Houston, and Galveston if necessary, and find some way of enlisting, he paying one-half the expense, which he did.

> So I boarded a flatcar at the appointed time, and in the course of several hours made Liberty; from there I pumped my way to Houston on a hand car.[6]

As a border state Texas escaped many of the ravages of war borne by her sister states of the Southern Confederacy. Although over 60,000 Texans served in the military forces of the Confederacy, and although her banners were carried on distant battlefields by such distinguished units as Hood's Brigade, Terry's Texas Rangers, Walker's Division, and Polignac's Brigade, most of the state escaped military invasion and was spared the pangs of destructive battle. This does not mean that the war had no effect on the state, however, as the four years of military hostilities caused a severe interruption in the everyday life of Texans during the conflict. Certainly this was most pronounced in the case of those 60,000 or more Texans who wore the gray and served on far-flung battlefields, but it was also true of those who remained within the state during the four years of war.

As the section of the state closest to the scene of the heaviest fighting, East Texas was probably affected more by the war than the rest of the state. Not only was this section the center of numerous governmental and military activities of the Trans-Mississippi Department as well as the Missouri government in exile, but also it was the area which received large numbers of refugees from the war-torn areas of Louisiana and Arkansas. In addition, it was the site of two major Confederate prison camps, Camp Groce near Hempstead and Camp Ford near Tyler, several iron foundries, several salt works, and ordnance works, and the most important military engagement fought in Texas during the Civil War — the battle of Sabine Pass.[7]

No area of East Texas life was more affected by the war than that of transportation. The outbreak of fighting stopped all railroad building for seven years and difficulties in maintaining rolling stock caused others to be abandoned.[8] So badly hurt were the Texas railroads that none of them paid dividends during the war. In one case, General John B. Magruder, district commander for Texas, tore up much of the Eastern Texas Road and the

Beaumont-Orange segment of the Texas & New Orleans Road for coastal fortifications. And in another instance several miles of track between Swanson's Landing and Jonesville in East Texas were taken up and relaid eastward from Marshall to Waskom for military purposes.[9]

Stage coach lines continued to operate in all of the state but the coaches were usually overcrowded and behind schedule. Colonel Arthur Fremantle of the British Coldstream Guards who toured Texas during the Civil War noted that the coach he rode near Houston contained eighteen passengers by the end of the trip and that the coach he rode in Northeast Texas had to stop just outside the town of Rusk so that all passengers could get out and cover the biggest holes in the bridge with planks.[10]

Accommodations for the traveler in Civil War East Texas were sometimes poor. Chaplain Nicholas Davis reported many kindnesses were shown in 1861 while troops of Hood's Brigade were camped along Buffalo Bayou at Houston,[11] and Private Dunbar Affleck, traveling from his home near Brenham to Houston, stayed with a lady who gave him a lunch and invited him to return, saying her home was always open to soldiers.[12] But most travelers were not so fortunate. Kate Stone, a young refugee from Louisiana, reported that on her trip from Monroe, Louisiana to Lamar County in the Red River country she had to camp along the way. Her experience in East Texas led her to write a relative in Louisiana "never to come to Texas for pleasure, but if forced to come to cover herself with a thin coat of tar to protect herself from the myriads of insects along the road." She went on to declare that East Texas was the headquarters for "ticks, redbugs, fleas by the millions, and snakes gliding through the grass by the hundreds" and to report that she was always afraid at night she would "feel the sting of a tarantula or centipede."[13] On another trip from Tyler to Lamar County, she and her mother spent the night at a house that was pretty and white on the outside, but filthy on the inside. She reported that they "tried to eat without seeing or tasting and to sleep without touching the bed." They were given coffee, "a horrid decoction of burnt wheat and milk without sugar, in saucers and water in the halves of broken bottles." Kate concluded that she had surely "found the dark corner of the Confederacy."

Traveling in Civil War East Texas presented many special problems. There were so many refugees and travelers that a Houston editor wrote that the hotels were filled from attic to basement. He went on to state that "Texas may be sparsely populated, but we have seen enough people during the last few weeks to whip any Yankee force that may be sent here."[15] Usually it was necessary for the traveler to share hotel rooms that often lacked in comforts and cleanliness. Colonel Fremantle found Houston crowded with refugees from Galveston but reported that as a great favor to a foreign visitor he was allowed a bed to himself; all "other beds in the room had two occupants each," he noted.[16] At Crockett, however, Fremantle was not so fortunate. Here he shared a bed with a Louisiana judge, a bed which Fremantle found so filthy that he and the judge slept with their boots on. In Rusk Fremantle was able to get a single bed through the influence of a friend, but noted it was not "inviting enough to induce me to remove my clothes."[17] He did, however, find the food in east Texas satisfactory, reporting that he was served pork or bacon, bread made with Indian corn and "a peculiar mixture called Confederate coffee, made of rye, meal, Indian corn or sweet potatoes."

Train travelers shared some of the same difficulties as those who journeyed by stage. An army surgeon traveling from Houston to Beaumont in 1864 reported there was no fire in the railroad cars and "to make matters worse the cars ran over a cow & run off the track which made us in the night getting to Beaumont." Arrival in the city brought no improvement in his comfort — he found the townspeople would not get up, so he had to "hunt up wood & make a fire" and then spread his blankets on the floor of the station and sleep there.[18]

Those who stayed at home had as many, if not more, problems as the traveler. In nearly every community there was a shortage of houses; this was especially true of areas along the coast and along the Louisiana and

Arkansas state lines as thousands of refugees poured into the interior. Thomas North, a traveler from the Midwest, reported there was a general evacuation of non-combatants from Galveston Island resulting in a "general stampede of people and valuables up country."[19] And Mary Elizabeth Massey in her recent study of Confederate refugees notes that thousands came from Louisiana and Arkansas to East Texas to escape the ravages of war.[20] Tyler, Rusk, Marshall, and Corsicana were the principal depots for refugees in the interior, while Houston was the main refugee center along the coast.

The addition of thousands of refugees and the effect of the Union blockade caused a number of shortages in East Texas. Although cases of serious food shortages were rare, there were shortages of many specific commodities, especially those which formerly had been imported. Coffee was a particularly cherished item that was always in demand. Colonel Fremantle noted "the loss of coffee afflicts the Confederates even more than the loss of spirits." He also observed that "they exercise their ingenuity in devising substitutes, which are not generally very successful."[21] Among the many substitutes used, corn coffee was favored in East Texas.

Substitutes for tea were made from various types of leaves, especially the yaupon which some said tasted almost like imported Asian tea. Not all were so impressed with yaupon tea, however; one Union prisoner of war who tasted it declared it produced "a burning sensation" in the stomach. And another observer referred to its "unpleasant medical effects."[22]

The shortage of manufactured goods grew as the war continued. Most manufactured goods, especially clothing, had been imported from Europe or the North before the war. Now, East Texans had to produce their own goods. The largest cloth factory developed during the war was at the state penitentiary at Huntsville, where over 200 convicts turned out nearly 6,000 yards of cloth daily, but throughout East Texas women were urged to spin their own cloth, an art commonly practiced earlier but which had become less common in the 1850s. Newspaper editors encouraged home weaving, competition between the women was encouraged, and Governor Francis R. Lubbock was inaugurated in a homespun suit in 1861.[23]

Shoes were also badly needed. A news item in the Galveston paper for October, 1862, describes how one man tanned his own leather by putting the hides in ashes and water to remove the hair; they were then put in a solution of oak bark that had been boiled and cooled until warm. According to the writer the leather produced was soft and pliant, but evidently home tanning was never too popular as prices of shoes and boots continued to rise in East Texas.[24]

War time needs stimulated some industries already established and encouraged the development of others. Salt works in Cherokee, Van Zandt and Smith counties did a thriving business. There was an ordnance works at Tyler, jug factories in Rusk and Henderson counties, and iron foundries in Anderson, Cass, Henderson, Harrison, Cherokee, Marion, Nacogdoches, and Smith counties.[25]

East Texans were called on to use their ingenuity to find substitutes for many small personal items that were formerly imported. The editor of the Clarksville **Standard** described a substitute for soda which could easily be produced. This consisted of adding ashes of corn cobs to boiling water, allowing to stand a minute, then pouring off the liquid which could be used at once with an acid such as sour milk or vinegar. According to the editor "it makes a bread as light almost as snow."[26] Another editor noted that a homemade glue was "far superior to the common imported glue," but failed to describe how it could be made.[27] Substitutes for ink were easily found and made of the bark of dogwood, oak, pomegranate rinds, elderberries, or green persimmons.[28] Shoe blacking was also scarce during the war but one writer told of making blacking from chinaberries and in her diary Kate Stone described a homemade blacking just as shiny as the old blacking.[29]

Just as East Texans had to improvise and find substitutes for food and everyday items, so, too, did they find substitutes for medicines, and again they received assistance from the newspaper editors. Most medicines had been imported before secession and there were never enough available during the war. Quinine was almost indispensable, since malaria and other fevers were common in the lower South.[30] Many substitutes were attempted; the dogwood berry seemed to be superior to most. One newspaper editor claimed it had been used successfully a number of times and urged Texans to gather and dry the berries for future use. Another editor included a remedy for the "flux," which he stated could be cured by drinking at intervals sage tea with red pepper stirred into it.[31]

Fortunately, the general health of East Texans was fairly good during the war except for the usual fevers in the coastal areas. In September, 1862, 50-60 cases of yellow fever were reported at Sabine Pass, of which 25 patients died; eight cases were reported at Beaumont and one at Orange. There were 30-40 cases of yellow fever in Houston and 8-10 deaths by the end of October, 1862. Again in September, 1864, yellow fever was reported in epidemic at Galveston and Houston; quite a few had died and all men on furloughs were ordered to remain at home. Small pox was also prevalent in the coastal area; in December, 1863, residents of Houston were urged to take every precaution against the disease. And an army surgeon at Beaumont reported a number of cases of "Congestion" in the summer of 1864.[32]

Although there were hardships, shortages, and epidemics during the war, there were gayer times as well. In the early part of the war the traditional spas and watering places continued to receive visitors. The management of the Dalby Springs Hotel in Bowie County, for example, continued to operate and advertise for visitors during the summer season of 1861.[33] And the **Dallas Herald** in July, 1861, announced the opening of a new watering place, "Pleasant Springs" in Grimes County. According to the editor of the **Herald** the "accomodations are excellent" and the waters "possess curative properties second to none in the State."[34]

In the towns there were theaters, concerts, military balls, and benefit shows staged for the aid for refugees and orphans. Many towns had soldier's aid societies which provided entertainment and dances to raise funds to aid Confederate soldiers and their families.[33] Houston even held a children's fair for the benefit of the soldier's home and according to the editor of the Telegraph raised $1,000.[36]

One new form of entertainment was provided by Union prisoners. An account is given by one who was captured near Boston in East Texas, a town which he described as a "hard place" and one in which shooting scrapes were commonplace. According to his account the presence of Union prisoners was a novelty and their stay at the courthouse was "a source of interest and entertainment" for the citizens who came to see them and ask questions.[37]

In areas near army camps in East Texas there was more amusement than usual. Horse races, dances, and dinners were extended by the local citizenry to Confederate officers and enlisted men alike. One cavalryman, Private Dunbar Affleck of Brenham, who was stationed near Mt. Zion late in the war, wrote to his mother that there was one "frolic and dinner" after another and after several weeks in the area reported "I want now to leave this place, and go over on the Brazos as soon as possible, the people here intend giving us another frolic next week if we remain here that long, but I hope for that reason we wont stay, because I never was so worn out in my life before."[38] Affleck also reported that a new sport, gander pulling, was a common amusement in East Texas, although some of "the ladies did not like pulling at the old gander, it was too cruel for them."[39]

The lengthening shadow of military defeat on fields of distant battle, however, had its effect upon life in East Texas. Every Confederate defeat beyond the borders of Texas — Price's cavalry disaster in Missouri in late 1864, Sherman's capture of Savannah in December — caused increased anxiety in the state. Newspaper editorials in early 1865 urged East Texans to remain firm and General John B. Magruder, commander of the district of Texas, called upon his soldiers to stand by their colors. Governor Pendleton Murrah asked Texans to keep up the struggle and General Edmund Kirby Smith, commander of the Trans-Mississippi Department, declared he would fight on.[40] But news of Lee's surrender in April, followed by that of Joe Johnston in North Carolina, made further resistance appear futile. On May 15, troops at Galveston mutinied and took off for home. At the same time other garrisons along the coast showed an open disregard for discipline. Again newspapers called for discipline and both Magruder and Smith tried to restore order, but it was too late.[41] When Smith reached Huntsville on his trip southward to restore order he found mobs of soldiers crowding the road with no thought but to return home. By the time he reached Houston he found himself a general without an army. In late May, Smith heard that his chief of staff had already surrendered the Trans-Mississippi Department at New Orleans and that the formal terms of surrender were being brought to Galveston for his signature. There was little he could now do. On June 2, with "Prince John" Magruder at his side, Smith boarded the Union ship in Galveston harbor and signed the surrender terms.[42] Ahead were the long months of Reconstruction. The Civil War was over.

Notes

1. Texas was represented in the Montgomery convention before the vote of the people was canvassed by the secession convention but her delegates were not "officially" seated until March 2. The formal ratification of the permanent Confederate Constitution was completed by the Texas convention on March 23. See Journal of the Secession Convention of Texas, Edited from the Original by Ernest W. Winkler (Austin, 1912), 233, and Charles Robert Lee, Jr., The Confederate Constitutions (Chapel Hill, 1963), 53, 87, 131.

2. The term "East Texas" here is used to designate some thirty-six counties in the eastern portion of the state bounded on the west by Red River, Titus, Wood, Smith, Anderson, Leon, Madison, Grimes, Harris and Galveston counties. See The Handbook of Texas (2 vols.; Austin, 1952), I, 534-535.

3. Quoted in Earl W. Fornell, The Galveston Era (Austin, 1961), 291.

4. See Allan C. Ashcraft, "East Texas in the Election of 1860 and the Secession Crisis," **East Texas Historical Journal**, I (July, 1963), 12-23, and Stephen B. Oates, "Texas Under the Secessionists," **Southwestern Historical Quarterly**, LXVII (October, 1963), 171-72.

5. William W. Heartsill, **Fourteen Hundred and Ninety-One Days in the Confederate Army; or, Camp Life, Day by Day, of the W. P. Lane Rangers from April 19, 1861 to May 20, 1865** (Reprint ed. by Bell. I. Wiley; Jackson, Tennessee, Inc., 1954), 2-5.

6. William A. Fletcher, **Rebel Private, Front and Rear** (Reprint ed. by Bell I. Wiley; Austin, 1954), 6-7. Fletcher's difficulties did not end in Houston. He found no companies recruiting there and had to return to Liberty, where he was accepted into a Confederate unit. For other descriptions of recruiting and enrolling troops in East Texas see **Clarksville Standard,** May 18, May 22, June 1, 1861, and the **Dallas Herald,** June 19 and July 17, 1861.

7. For governmental activities see William R. Geise, "Missouri's Confederate Capital in Marshall, Texas," **Southwestern Historical Quarterly**, LXVI (October, 1962), 201-202. For military prisons see Leon Mitchell, Jr., "Camp Groce: Confederate Military Prison," **ibid.**, LXVII (July, 1963), 15-21, and "Camp Ford: Confederate Military Prison," **ibid.**, LXVI (July, 1962), 1-16; and F. Lee Lawrence and Robert W. Glover, **Camp Ford, C.S.A.** (Austin, 1964). For the battle of Sabine Pass see **Official Records of the War of Rebellion** (130 vols.; Washington, 1880-1891), Series I, Vol. XXVIV, Pt. 1, 309-312; Andrew Forest Muir, "Dick Dowling and the Battle of Sabine Pass," **Civil War History**, IV (December, 1958), 399-428; and Alwyn Barr, "Texas Coastal Defense, 1861-1865," **Southwestern Historical Quarterly**, XLV (July, 1961), 24-27.

8. William B. Bizzell, **Rural Texas** (New York, 1924), 235-36; Andrew Forest Muir, "Railroads Come to Houston, 1857-1861," **Southwestern Historical Quarterly**, LXIV (July, 1960), 63; James F. Doster, "Were the Southern Railroads Destroyed by War?" **Civil War History**, VII (September, 1961), 320.

9 .Robert C. Black III, **The Railroads of the Confederacy** (Chapel Hill, 1952), 299; Sallie M. Lentz, "Highlights of Early Harrison County," **Southwestern Historical Quarterly**, LXI (October, 1957), 251.

10. Lieutenant Colonel Arthur James Lyon Fremantle, **The Fremantle Diary, Being the Journal of Lieutenant Colonel James Arthur Lyon Fremantle, Coldstream Guards, on His Three Months in the Southern States** (Reprint ed. by Walter Lord; Boston, 1954), 63.

11. Nicholas A. Davis, **Chaplain Davis and Hood's Texas Brigade** (ed. by Donald E. Everett; San Antonio, 1960), 3.

12. Dunbar Affleck to Mr. and Mrs. Thomas Affleck, December 15, 1863, Letters in possession of Mr. T. D. Affleck, Galveston, Texas.

13. **Brokenburn: The Journal of Kate Stone, 1861-1868** (ed. by John Q. Anderson; Baton Rouge, 1955), 224.

14. Ibid., 237.

15. Houston Tri-Weekly Telegraph, June 23, 1862, quoted in Mary Elizabeth Massey, Ersatz in the Confederacy (Columbia, 1952), 103.
16. Fremantle Diary, 51.
17. Ibid., 61-62.
18. "Letters from the Confederate Medical Service in Texas, 1863-1865," ed. by Frank E. Vandiver, Southwestern Historical Quarterly, LV (January, 1952), 392-93.
19. Thomas North, Five Years in Texas; or, What You Did Not Hear During the War From January 1861 to January 1866 (Cincinnati, 1871), 106.
20. Mary Elizabeth Massey, Refugee Life in the Confederacy (Baton Rouge, 1964), 63-64, 90-94, 123-24. Kate Stone, herself a refugee, reports in her diary that there was considerable prejudice existing in some places toward the refugees. Brokenburn, 250, 275. Not all East Texans felt this way, however. See an editorial welcoming Louisiana refugees in Houston Tri-Weekly Telegraph, January 28, 1865.
21. Fremantle Diary, 62.
22. Charles C. Nott, Sketches in Prison Camps: A Contribution of Sketches of the War (New York, 1865), 119-21.
23. Galveston Weekly News, September 24, 1862; Massey, Ersatz in the Confederacy, 88-89.
24. Galveston Weekly News, September 22, 1862; February 11, 1863; May 20, 1863.
25. Robert L. Jones, "The First Iron Furnace in Texas," Southwestern Historical Quarterly, LXIII (October, 1959), 288; Ollie Singletary, "A History of the Iron Industry of Northeast Texas," Unpublished M.A. thesis, East Texas State College, 1951, pp. 25-39; Dorman H. Winfrey, A History of Rusk County, Texas (Waco, 1961), 62; Lentz, "Highlights of Early Harrison County," Southwestern Historical Quarterly, LXI, 252-53; William A. Albaugh III, Tyler, Texas, CSA (Harrisburg, Penna, 1958), 11-29; T. C. Richardson, East Texas, Its History and Its Makers (4 vols; New York, 1940), I, 204; Henderson Times, November 21, 1863; Clarksville Standard, December 31, 1861.
26. Clarksville Standard, July 7, 1862.
27. Houston Tri-Weekly Telegraph, January 11, 1865.
28. Galveston Weekly News, September 24, 1862.
29. Ibid., January 27, 1864; Brokenburn, 332. Where regular manufactured items were available prices were frequently prohibitive. Kate Stone reported that calico cost $6 a yard in Tyler in 1863. A pen knife sold for $25 and a deck of playing cards $5. An army surgeon stationed at Beaumont related that tobacco cost $30 per pound and a chicken cost $10. "Letters from the Confederate Medical Service in Texas, 1863-1865," Southwestern Historical Quarterly, LX, 459, 469.
30. John Q. Anderson, A Texas Surgeon in the C.S.A. (Tuscaloosa, 1957), 19.

31. Galveston Weekly News, September 10, 1862; July 30, 1862; October 28, 1862.

32. Ibid., September 17, October 15, October 29, 1862; October 28, 1863; Mrs. Thomas Affleck to Dunbar Affleck, September 23, 1864; and "Letters from the Confederate Medical Service in Texas, 1863-1865," Southwestern Historical Quarterly, LV, 463.

33. Clarksville Standard, July 20, 1861.

34. Dallas Herald, July 3, 1861.

35. Brokenburn, 320; "Letters from the Confederate Medical Service in Texas, 1863-1865," Southwestern Historical Quarterly, LV, 472; Henderson Times, December 19, 1863, December 17, 1864.

36. Houston Tri-Weekly Telegraph, March 21, 1865, LV, 472; Henderson Times, December 19, 1863, December 17, 1864.

37. S. A. Swiggert, The Bright Side of Prison Life, Experiences, in Prison and Out, of an Involuntary Sojurner in Rebeldom (Baltimore, 1897), 97.

38. Dunbar Affleck to Mrs. Thomas Affleck, February 20, 1865.

39. Dunbar Affleck to Mrs. Thomas Affleck, February 16, 1865.

40. Houston Tri-Weekly Telegraph, January 5, 1865, March 11, 1865; Oates, "Texas Under the Secessionists," Southwestern Historical Quarterly, LXVII, 210.

41. Houston Tri-Weekly Telegraph, April 17, 1865.

42. The last months of the Confederacy are ably covered in Oates, "Texas Under the Secessionists," Southwestern Historical Quarterly, LXVII, 210-12.

8

Black Texans During Reconstruction: First Freedom

by
James Smallwood

James Smallwood is director of the Will Rogers Research Project and Assistant Professor of History at Oklahoma State University, Stillwater, Oklahoma.

8

After the defeat of the Confederacy, Texas became a scene of confusion for whites and blacks alike, but civil government resumed in the state on July 21, 1865, when Andrew Johnson's appointee, Unionist A. J. Hamilton, arrived in Galveston to assume the governorship. In August he began appointing fellow Unionists and some ex-Confederates to state, district, county, and precinct offices. By the end of the month, civil government functioned in eighty counties, but major adjustments remained.[1] Authorities found themselves confronted with many problems of which the most enduring involved the question of black status. Although most white Texans hoped this would not be the case, Union victory in war carried with it emancipation for slaves. Many questions arose: How would Negroes respond to their new "condition?" How would whites react? What degree of control over black labor, if any, would the national government allow native Anglos? Would blacks have the same political rights and legal status as whites? These issues absorbed Texans in the post-war era.

After General Gordon Granger delivered the Texas Emancipation Proclamation in Galveston on June 19,[2] the immediate reaction of the slaves varied. A minority temporarily became confused. Will Adams reported that on the James Davis plantation in San Jacinto county, "there was lots of crying and weeping when they were set free. Lot's [sic] of them didn't want to be free because they knew nothing and had nowhere to go."[3] On other plantations and farms, after masters made the emancipation announcement, some ex-slaves shocked and unsure of their new status, still asked for passes when they left.[4]

For some freedmen joy replaced temporary confusion. Blacks turned many plantations into scenes of jubilation and alternately sang, danced, and prayed.[5] Some became overjoyed simply because they believed freedom meant "no more whippings."[6] The reaction of Harriet, a domestic slave hired out to Amelia Barr of Austin, perhaps typified that of many Negroes. After the local sheriff read Granger's proclamation, Amelia informed Harriet that she was free. Afterwards, Harriet

> darted to her child, and throwing it high, shrieked hysterically, 'Tamar, you are free. You are free, Tamar!' She did not at that supreme moment think of herself. Freedom was for her child; she looked in its face, at its hands, at its feet. It was a new baby to her — a free baby.[7]

Like Harriet, most slave parents probably thought of their children first, wanting them to have the same benefits as slaveholders' children — schooling, attractive clothes, sufficient food, and exemption from work. A majority of the bondsmen, however, suffered no great confusion as a result of emancipation, and if they felt joy, they restrained their enthusiasm. Most quietly planned to leave their masters as soon as possible.

To the slaves, emancipation had many potential meanings. Generally, blacks expected the same freedoms that Anglos enjoyed, with the same prerogatives and opportunities. In terms of priorities, educated Negroes emphasized the importance of full and immediate political and civil rights while the masses advocated land redistribution and educational opportunity. Blacks believed that political rights would help protect them from social and economic discrimination and that land redistribution would provide a stable base for future progress. On a more common level, Negroes also hoped that emanicipation meant a new home, a new job, a new social life, complete religious freedom, and the right of unrestricted travel — to seek better employment or to locate lost family members. Emancipation had yet another definition for black women who had been field hands. They believed that they, like white mistresses, should now be exempt from field labor, that they should engage in housework only, reserving free time for visiting and for shopping.[8]

Early in 1865, even before the army and the Freedmen's Bureau could provide assistance, blacks began trying to reorder their lives and fulfill the aspirations of freedom. Wishing to secure an education for themselves and their children, for example, many freedmen bought primers and writing slates and tried to learn how to read and write. Then they organized makeshift schools and supported teachers with moderate tuition and presents of food after the harvest. Just as they began establishing schools, blacks quickly began founding their own religious institutions. They withdrew from native white churches and joined the "northern wing" of established Anglo churches or organized their own services. Negroes also developed a more diversified social life which usually centered around their schools and churches. Church and school-sponsored picnics, dances, and fairs along with regular Sabbath services represented a few of the limited recreational outlets available to blacks. Equally important to the new freedmen was their search for lost relatives which usually began at first opportunity. In most cases, however, blacks had to wait for the aid of the bureau before they could locate family members who had been "lost" because of family splitting before emancipation.[9]

Accepting the aid of sincere Unionists, blacks who successfully made the transition from slavery to freedom

131

tried to help those more unfortunate. In Houston Reverend Elias Dibble organized a mutual aid society to help sick or distressed Negroes. With members paying a rather large $2.50 initiation fee and $.25 weekly dues, the society quickly collected an $80 relief fund. In San Antonio Nace Duval, preacher and barber, performed a valuable service for fellow blacks when he established an employment bureau. Many newly emerging black congregations also founded benevolent agencies to assist destitutes. Likewise, some Unionists, particularly Germans, took an interest in Negro welfare. In addition to offering protection to hunted freedmen, Louis Constant ran a combination boarding house, relief station, and employment service for ex-slaves.[10]

To test their new freedom and to escape hated reminders of slavery, those Negroes who had a place to go gathered their belongings and left first while the aged and infirm tended to leave last. On the William Ballinger farm three younger slaves immediately left, but six who had no place to go continued to work for Ballinger for monthly wages. Only freedmen who had had kindly owners voluntarily remained at their old jobs because most ex-slaveholders tended to treat blacks as if they were still slaves. Rather than accept this, Negroes left. Further, those who remained usually did so only for a few months. Yet comparisons of the 1860 and 1870 census statistics reveals that no massive shifting of Negro population occurred. The percentage of black population remained relatively stable in all parts of the state. Many blacks who left old masters went only a few miles before hiring out to a new employer. Others, particularly those whom whites brought to Texas during the war, left the state to return to old homes and to rejoin their families.[11] Still others flocked to the nearest town.

According to one witness of what appeared to be a mass black migration to urban centers, the ex-slaves wanted "to get closer to freedom, so they'd know what it was — like it was a place or a city."[12] Migrants became so numerous that they filled the roads to such towns as Houston, San Antonio, Gonzales, and Jefferson. Austin suffered temporary problems in public health and sanitation because of overcrowding. In the urban centers some blacks passed their time in idleness or in gaming, trying to enjoy their new freedom. But historians who have argued that "all" or "most" Negroes refused to work and led a wayward type of existence in the cities probably exaggerated. Rather, what whites called laziness usually amounted to a typical worker's rebellion against unreasonable hours and wages and became a way of demanding rest and enjoyment. Whites nevertheless expected the worst from freedom, and this general attitude allowed them to believe almost any rumor directed against Negroes. In 1866 a Freedmen's Bureau agent in Bastrop heard reports that blacks in Austin refused to work and simply wandered around. Austin agent Byron Porter, however, wondered how his counterpart in Bastrop received such misinformation. The great majority of Negroes in Austin, Porter maintained, had jobs. In urban centers, then, most blacks sought employment. Some hired out as domestics or day laborers. Catering to the new black population in the towns, some opened business establishments such as barber shops, grocery stores, and shoe shops. Others found benevolent military commands like those in Houston who created jobs by instigating temporary relief projects.[13]

Black population growth in urban areas continued through the late 1860s to outstrip white increases, but many freedmen soon discovered that towns were not the havens they sought. Urban Anglos feared blacks, believing that their increased numbers would cause more crime. Further, white employers, believing absolutely in black inferiority, refused to allow freedmen the dignity accorded white labor. Still, blacks found themselves treated as slaves. Refusing to hire the new freedmen, other employers replaced them with white labor even though Anglos demanded higher wages.[14] White politicos applauded this trend. The growth of an Anglo mechanic class was necessary, said the editor of the **Houston Telegraph**, or "the ignorant race" would swamp Houston and retard its development. Later, the editor noted with satisfaction that whites had replaced blacks as drivers of a majority of the city's drays. The editor of the **Hunts-**

ville Item noted similar trends occuring in his town and expressed approval.[15]

Trying to encourage their removal, some city governments also discriminated against freedmen. The Galveston mayor harassed blacks whenever they tried to gather for social events. Although military authorities always gave blacks permission to conduct meetings or hold balls, the mayor broke up any gathering and fined supposed organizers, justifying his action with an apparently little-used local permit ordinance.[16] Victims of white discrimination and of what became a glutted labor market, many blacks returned to the rural area which they regarded as home because they knew it well. But most found that conditions in the countryside were in many ways worse than in the cities.

Some Negroes in rural areas found the transition to freedom particularly difficult because of the immediate reactions of their masters. Despite the fact that most farms and plantations needed laborers, a minority of owners — on first hearing of Granger's proclamation — took action that defied economic logic, relieving slaves of their jobs and telling them to get off the land. Ex-masters dismissed some blacks because they were purported to be bad influences on other freedmen. Thomas Greer of Madison County told his slaves to get out, saying that he would horsewhip any "nigger" he found on his place after the next sunrise.[17] Many freedmen, such as Toby Jones, reported that "they turned us out like a bunch of stray dogs, with no homes, no clothes, no nothing."[18] The blacks who had been turned out had no choice but to wander around, looking for work.

Some ex-slaves became victims of early Klan-like conspiracies. A large group of white citizens in Freestone County emphatically passed a general resolution in late 1865 vowing to hire no blacks and to whip any freedman who tried to contract with Anglos. Whites who violated the resolution might first only be warned but, on second offense, would be whipped or hanged.[19] Some ex-masters, extremely disturbed by emancipation and not content to deny blacks work, decided that slaves would be better off dead than free. By poisoning slave water wells, those masters reportedly killed scores of Negroes before they could escape from the old plantations.[20]

Slaves who were driven from the land found the first steps toward freedom painful. Some joined the migration to towns where they sought not just work but military protection from further abuse. Others relied solely on themselves and resorted to a most primitive type of existence. Unable to buy land, unwilling to accept semi-slavery under white employers, some squatted on unworked land and, using sticks as tools, planted crops. They supplemented their diet by fishing and by hunting — with bows and arrows — and made clothes from animal skins. Despite black efforts to provide for themselves, starvation became rife in some Texas counties, particularly in the north and northeast; to get food, some Negroes resorted to thievery.[21] So difficult was the plight of freedmen that Elige Divison could only comment, "if the woods were not full of wild game, all us Negroes would have starved to death."[22] And blacks like Davison could expect little help. The Freedmen's Bureau, the agency Congress established to aid blacks, did not begin to function in Texas until September 1865 and remained hopelessly undermanned until it finally was removed from the state in 1870.

Most former slaveowners did not turn the new freedmen off the land, but they, like most other whites, maintained an attitude not conducive to black freedom. Only briefly, just after the South's defeat, did white Texans adopt an apparently moderate attitude, one encouraged perhaps by their uncertainty regarding the kind of treatment that federal forces of occupation would mete out. Further, if they acted in a conciliatory manner, they believed that President Andrew Johnson's lenient Reconstruction policy would yet allow them to control the freedmen. Correspondents for various Texas newpapers reported that most planters and farmers quietly resigned themselves to the Union victory and black emancipation, freeing slaves and coming to terms with them. The citizens of some towns even passed resolutions vowing full cooperation with the federal government. Yet such mass displays of loyalty proved misleading. If a majority of whites at first appeared conciliatory, if newspapers advocated moderation, they did so only because they wanted to remove the necessity of a lengthy military occupation of the state.[21]

Even after the Union government made known its determination to end slavery, a majority of white Texans quickly reaffirmed their belief in white supremacy. As William Ballinger asserted even before Kirby Smith's surrender, Anglo Texans would always "remain Southern in their feelings."[24] After the war, whites clung to the "lost cause," sometimes making up new "Rebel ditties" like "Conquered Banner" and "Faded Gray Jacket" to glorify the Old South.[25] Whites feared that freedom for blacks implied equality of the races, an idea that most refused to accept. Many believed the Negro race so inferior that amalgamation represented the only way to uplift it; thus, arguments against black equality often focused on the question of racial mixing. Whites feared that granting the Negroes political and legal rights ultimately would lead to social equality which in turn would lead to amalgamation; hence, many Anglos opposed giving any rights to Negroes.[26] If freedmen received any rights, "then the kinky hair," lamented one editor, "the mellow eye, the artistic nose, the seductive lips, the ebony skin and bewildering odor will be ours, all ours, ours, ours."[27] Like most white Texans, the editor of the **San Antonio Daily Herald** joined the critics, telling the black man that "this is our government and country, and not his, if he don't like it, he is at liberty to seek another."[28]

In addition to objecting to black freedom for racial reasons, most Anglos stressed economic arguments, using the complaint that unless compelled, freedmen would not work. Whites attributed this alleged reluctance about work to the irresponsible, lazy, and ignorant "nature" of the Negro and to the "foolish" notion that Yankees would give blacks land. Anglos apparently failed to remember that the hot summer, even in the antebellum period, traditionally had been a time of less work. Moreover, blacks moved about immediately after emancipation to test their freedom, to escape hated masters, and to find new jobs or lost family members. Whites attributed the migration to pure wanderlust which, they believed, proved their point: free black labor was unstable.[29]

Whites resisted Negro emancipation for yet other reasons. Some believed that unless blacks were controlled they would take revenge on the society which had enslaved them. This fear became especially pronounced in areas of large Negro population. In Harrison County, where freedmen numbered about 60 percent of the total population, Anglos around Marshall set up contingency plans to protect themselves from a rebellion. Even in areas of smaller black population, whites did not feel safe unless they placed some restrictions on freedmen. In San Antonio the city council adopted a nine o'clock curfew for any type of black meeting.[30] The belief that blacks committed most crimes further stimulated white fears of rebellion. Anglo criminals helped reinforce this belief by committing night robberies while disguised as Negroes. A group of whites in black-face beat and robbed a German named Homeyer in his home near Brenham, but they proved to be inept for Homeyer later identified them as Anglos.[31]

So strong was the white desire to "keep blacks in their place" that when they realized abolition to be a fact, Anglos took overt action which necessitated strong countermeasures by the federal goverment. A one-sided guerilla war with stong racial overtones developed in Texas and continued to influence the entire course of events in the attempted Reconstruction of the State. The war took many forms, with black people the usual targets for violence perpetuated by whites. The violence sometimes seemed casual, with Anglos having no apparent motive except to chastise "uppity" blacks who were guilty of nothing more than exercising their new freedom. At other times the violence became well directed, with planters using force to keep Negroes in illegal bondage. Disgruntled whites did not confine their wrath to blacks but also identified Anglo Unionists as targets because to varying degrees they supported Negro rights. Most white Texans committed no outrages, but many actively conspired with those who did, by hiding them from the authorities and by refusing to testify against them. Violence against blacks and Unionists erupted sporadically throughout the state. Although outrages occurred more frequently in the interior at isolated points unprotected by federal forces, white men murdered and whipped blacks even in areas of military occupation. Federal officials reported that at times entire counties went out of control.[32]

In many areas trouble began with early military occupation. Whites immediately demonstrated their hostility for the government. In Millican when Unionists raised the United States' flag, Colonel W. B. Lowery pulled it down. At Weatherford ex-Confederates took the flag from the court house and tore it to pieces. Through 1865 reports came to Governor Hamilton from all over the state informing him that disloyal factions just waited for their "chance" to "get at" freedmen and Unionists.[33]

While demonstrating contempt for the Union, some Anglos also inflicted barbarities on freedmen. Whites killed Negroes for the most trivial offenses. In Huntsville during a celebration of emancipation by freedmen, one local white rode into the midst of a jubilee and, wielding a knife, disemboweled a black woman whose body was then pitched into a wagon and taken away.[34] An historian listed other "reputedly assigned reasons" for murder:

> freedmen did not remove his hat when he passed him (a white man); negro would not allow himself to be whipped; freedman would not allow his wife to be whipped by a white man; he was carrying a letter to a Freedman's Bureau official; kill negroes to see them kick; wanted to thin out niggers a little; didn't hand over his money quick enough; wouldn't give up his whiskey flask.[35]

Anglos beat blacks for almost any offense, including indications of freedmen that they were in fact emancipated. If Negroes did not show due deference in all matters involving whites, they faced punishment. Beginning after emancipation and continuing throughout Reconstruction, Anglos complained about impudent behavior by Negroes, failing to understand that blacks needed to test their freedom. Further, white men clung to the sexual mores of the antebellum period, which included exploitation of black women. Freedmen Bureau records contained frequent complaints of rape or attempted rape of Negro women by white men.[36]

The congressional investigation of 1866 produced statistics and testimony proving that such violent acts had become a common theme of early postwar race relations in Texas. From mid-1865 to early 1866, authorities issued 500 indictments for the murder of blacks by Anglos, but because of white attitudes no convictions resulted. Two Anglos killed a black domestic servant in Harrison County because she would not punish her child for stealing money. Lucy Grimes explained that the young child only played with the money, as one would with a toy. After hearing what they regarded as a "fishy" story, the men took the woman to a wooded area outside of Marshall, stripped her, and beat her to death. The murder went unpunished because the county judge refused to hear a complaint brought by a Negro, Lucy's older son.[37]

Some slaveholders who desperately wanted to control their labor force added to the violent atmosphere by refusing to free their chattels. Other owners merely followed a policy of drift, informing bondsmen of Granger's proclamation only after rumors of freedom became so strong that they could not be denied. Still others determined to get summer crops in before telling slaves of emancipation. This group usually tricked the freedmen into remaining at their jobs. Unscrupulous masters promised blacks full rations and a share of all crops — some even promised to give them small plots of land and livestock. After the harvest, most refused to honor their agreements and drove Negroes from the land.[38]

Some owners refused to free their bondsmen even after the harvest. Anderson Edwards remained a slave on the Rusk County plantation of Major Matt Gaud for one full year after Granger's proclamation. Saying that God "never did intend to free niggers," Gaud ignored the emancipation order until federal soldiers discovered his illegal actions and forced him to release Edwards and other slaves. One mistress kept a black woman chained to a loom to prevent her escape and continued to work her for "about" a year. In statements corroborated by white Unionists, other slaves reported similar experiences.[39]

In other instances, which occurred more frequently than many historians previously have supposed, owners kept blacks in illegal bondage not for just a few months but for years. After Union forces occupied Galveston, John E. Chisholm retreated deep into East Texas, settled, and worked his bondsmen as late as December 1866. On July 4, 1867, a group of freedmen in Austin encountered a black couple traveling with a white man who still held them in slavery. The freedmen's hostile protests influenced the immediate release of the couple. In the same month, the Freedman's Bureau agent in Austin reported that he recently had freed two girls whom planter William Greenwood had maintained in bondage. No one released the slaves of Alex Simpson, a horse thief, until he was hanged in 1868.[40] Certainly, most owners freed their slaves before 1868, but six months after Granger's proclamation, **Flake's Daily Bulletin** reported that some openly bragged that they continued to hold freedmen.[41]

Not all blacks submitted to illegal enslavement. When they learned that by right they should be free, they attempted to escape. As before the war, however, some whites used as much force as necessary to return escapees. Of his own personal knowledge, one Freedman's Bureau agent indicated that in the counties around Houston with considerable black population Anglos still used dog packs to capture runaways.[42] Further, whites sometimes killed escapees to discourage attempts by others. In Harrison County, most slaveholders freed their bondsmen before owners in neighboring Rusk County. Impatient for emancipation, slaves in Rusk County frequently ran away, trying to get over the county line, but many were killed in the attempt. "You could see lots of niggers hanging to trees in Sabine bottom right after freedom," asserted ex-slave Susan Merritt "because they [white men] caught them swimming across the Sabine River and shot them."⁴³

The Harrison County murders did not represent infrequent occurrences. A correspondent for **Flake's Daily Bulletin** reported that in "Middle Texas" as late as August, whites behaved in the same manner as those in Harrison. "More than twenty dead Negroes," he said "have [of late] drifted down the Brazos."⁴⁴ Moreover, four separate reports made by army officers in December, 1865 indicated that suppression and continued enslavement of blacks remained common throughout East and Central Texas. One federal official asserted that in the interior ex-masters still conducted their plantations as if the South had won the war. General E. M. Gregory, first commissioner of the Freedmen's Bureau in Texas, and General William E. Strong, inspector general of the bureau, held similar views. Gregory toured the region between the lower Colorado and the Brazos, while Strong toured the area between the Trintiy and the Neches. They found that wherever government troops were stationed Anglos behaved themselves but that where troops were absent some whites held blacks in bondage and treated them with utmost cruelty. Strong, who gave the more pessimistic report, recommended a military campaign to correct the situation. In conjunction with the tours of Gregory and Strong, I. J. W. Mintzer, surgeon-in-chief for the bureau, visited over 100 plantations along the Brazos and the Colorado and disgustedly reported that at will planters broke oral and written contracts with blacks. Whites who did not continue to hold Negroes in bondage sometimes exercised a more subtle type of control which proved equally effective. Anglos banded together and agreed not to hire any laborers without the consent of their previous employer.⁴⁵

While some ex-slaveholders circumvented federal laws by continuing to hold blacks after June 19, 1865, others reenslaved those who had been emancipated. Operating along the Texas coast, some whites gifted with beguiling stories convinced Negroes to board ships that would carry them to "a better place." Ship captains then took them to Cuba to sell them to "a better place." Ship captains, like David F. Portis of Austin County, decided to leave the United States and tried to force their exslaves to go with them. Leading a party of sixteen men, Portis confronted Louis Constant, German Unionist, and asked the whereabouts of a certain teenaged black male whom Portis intended to carry with him to Brazil. Constant knew where the freedman was hiding but refused to allow a search.[46]

As late as 1867 some white entrepreneurs evolved an elaborate plan that one witness called the "Brazilian emigration scheme." Allegedly, Anglos from the coast went into Smith County offering blacks work as boat hands. Eventually, the businessmen transported several hundred freedmen to the coast and divided them into crews. Ships then sailed, bound for New Orleans. Before reaching the port, whites put the blacks in chains. Captains then loaded the "cargo" aboard vessels bound for Brazil where the captives again would be enslaved.[47] As was obvious from the attitudes and actions of white Texans, the first few months of the new freedom found most blacks in a difficult situation.

Although the myth developed that the white South cared for the ex-slaves' welfare, kindness and concern may have been the exception rather than the rule. Yet freedmen could expect little relief from the still disorganized state government. Hamilton filled offices slowly and unknowingly appointed many unreconstructed rebels. Although other southern states held their constitutional conventions in the fall of 1865, he postponed the Texas convention until February 1866, explaining to President Johnson that he could not act more rapidly because whites refused to give freedmen their rights. In the interim, Hamilton took no positive action to settle the outstanding issues involving Negroes. He appealed publicly for racial conciliation, but in his November proclamation to freedmen he put little emphasis on their rights and instead stressed order, told Negroes to work, and tried to discourage rumors of land redistribution.[48]

The Texas Emancipation Proclamation guaranteed freedmen absolute equality in personal and property rights, but confusion resulted regarding the legal status of blacks. Many state judges like Hiram Christian, chief justice of Bell County, wrote Hamilton inquiring about the judicial rights of Negroes — could freedmen sue, complain against or testify against whites? The governor ruled that these were judicial questions to be settled by the courts. Some justices like C. C. Caldwell of Harris County instructed juries that perfect equality prevailed in all cases, but most judges in the state, following the old antebellum codes, refused to hear black complaints or testimony against Anglos. Furthermore, blacks usually faced exclusion from jury service. Even if courts accepted their testimony, white juries generally refused to convict fellow Anglos. So unfair was the system of justice that ranking federal officers labeled proceedings involving freedmen as complete farces.[49] Denied the protection of the Hamilton administration and the state courts, blacks continued to place faith in the federal government. Most believed that the Johnson government would implement a land redistribution program to give them economic security and that the army and the Freedmen's Bureau would protect them from further abuse. Negroes were disappointed on all counts.

Because the bureau did not enter the state until late 1865, the army shouldered the early responsibility for helping the Negroes adjust to freedom and for settling racial disputes. When General Granger issued the emancipation order, he initiated Texas Reconstruction. By his order blacks received equality in personal and property rights. At the same time, however, the general established a trend that later federal officials would follow. He showed more concern for order, stability, and the Negro labor "problem" than for black rights. He advised freedmen to sign labor contracts and to remain with their old masters. He warned that he would not allow blacks to collect at army posts nor would he support them in idleness. He also forbade Negroes to travel without passes from their employers.[50]

The attitude of a majority of military personnel limited the effectiveness of the army. White soldiers in the ranks felt prejudice against Negroes and did little to help or protect them. Occasionally, elements of the occupation force committed depredations on those who most needed protection. Blacks sometimes complained that soldiers, Negro and white, assaulted and robbed them. In Houston freedmen became so dissatisfied with troop behavior that in January 1866 they organized a vigilance committee numbering thirty to forty men and swore vengeance on the soldiers. A local war seemed unavoidable until a bureau agent managed to conciliate the freedmen.[51]

Prejudice permeated command positions as well as the lower ranks. Most officers made it no secret that they did not accept full Negro equality.[52] General William T. Sherman asserted that "the white men of this country will control it, and the Negroes, in mass, will occupy a subordinate place as a race."[53] Some commanders, of course, managed to overcome their prejudice, particularly those whose position necessitated frequent contact with freedmen. After gaining first-hand knowledge of the black plight, some officers changed their opinions of Negroes. They adopted attitudes which ranged from benevolent paternalism to outright sympathy.[54]

Even when prejudice did not limit the army, President Johnson's lenient Reconstruction plan did. Johnson, following his "easy" policy, did not envision a long occupation of Texas or the rest of the South. Nor did he foresee advancement of freedmen as one of the army's prime functions. To satisfy Johnson, former Confederate states had to acknowledge the end of slavery and accept federal law. The president intended to leave the black question to state authorities; he wanted rapid restoration and enjoined his military commanders from interfering with the organization and functioning of state governments.[55]

The impossibility of patrolling Texas with a limited force also hamstrung the army. Granger's original force of 1,800 men increased to 45,424 by September, partially because the Mexican Civil War made such a concentration necessary. But by January 1866 troop strength fell to 25,085. By February further reductions left approximately 5,000 soldiers in Texas. Furthermore, commanders were ordered to concentrate troops not along the coast or in the interior of the state but along the Rio Grande and in frontier outposts.⁵⁶ Thus undermanned in the areas of concentrated black population, the army could not provide the supervision needed to protect Negroes or to adjudicate racial disputes.

The Freedmen's Bureau finally began to function in Texas during September, 1865, when the first Assistant Commissioner for Texas, General E. M. Gregory, arrived in Galveston. Congress originally planned for the bureau to continue only one year after the end of the war. But when southern states passed the Black Codes and thus made known their determination to resist legal equality for Negroes, Congress renewed the bureau in 1866 over Johnson's veto and every year thereafter until 1870. As first conceived, the duties of the bureau varied. In Texas, because there were no abandoned lands to adjudicate, agents took legal jurisdiction over blacks if state courts appeared prejudicial and violated Negro rights and provided relief work if such aid seemed absolutely necessary. Bureau officials also encouraged blacks and their employers to honor labor contracts and sought to found and maintain bureau schools.⁵⁷

In areas other than labor supervision, the early work of the bureau achieved only moderate success. In extending immediate relief and medical aid to distressed freedmen, efforts fell far short of what blacks needed. The bureau issued relief rations to only sixty-four Negroes in 1865. In view of widespread want and some cases of starvation and in view of the increased rationing of 1866, it became obvious to Gregory's replacement, General J. B. Kiddoo, that the undermanned, underfinanced bureau reached only a small portion of the state's freedmen. The limited bureau established only one hospital, which never employed more than five doctors at any one time and was disbanded in September 1866.⁵⁸

Likewise, in its educational endeavors the bureau met with limited success. Edwin M. Wheelock, first superintendent of freedmen's schools in Texas, experienced difficulties in finding teachers and securing school supplies. He also found that the majority of white

Texans opposed black education, which presented problems that would continue throughout the Reconstruction period. Nevertheless, Wheelock established the first black school in the state, with an initial enrollment of eighty pupils, at Galveston in September. With only limited income from tuition charges of $1.50 per month from each student, bureau schools reached few Negroes in 1865. By October, Wheelock maintained five day, night, or Sabbath schools, with four teachers and an enrollment of 264. The bureau had increased the number to twelve, with nine teachers and 615 students by Christmas.[59]

To black Texans, the early absence of Freedmen's Bureau activity only mirrored similar developments which had occurred in the state in the first seven months after emancipation. Largely, Negroes found it possible to achieve their aspirations only in a most limited way. They hoped that freedom would bring economic and educational opportunity, religious autonomy, and family stability along with legal and political rights. True, they acquired more control over their family and social life and more freedom of movement and of expression, but only if they used their imagination could Negroes consider themselves free men. A majority of individual whites, the state government, the Johnson administration, and the army worked to limit black freedom. Whether they were city officials trying to force blacks out of urban areas, planters seeking to control Negro labor, or army officers wanting "order," Anglos discriminated against the new freedmen. Some whites who could not accept black emancipation committed barbarities on the Negroes, including murder whenever they wanted to "thin out niggers a little." Blacks found little relief. Self-help associations slowly developed, and a few Unionists offered aid. The early months of emancipation revealed the tensions between black hopes and white fears which would influence efforts by freedmen as they sought to fulfill aspirations in the decades to follow.

Notes

1. Ernest Wallace, **Texas in Turmoil** (Austin, 1965), 165.
2. Galveston Tri-Weekly News, June 30, 1865.
3. Statement of Will Adams, Federal Writers' Project, "A Folk History of Slavery in the United States from Interviews with Former Slaves" (Washington, 1941), Texas Narratives, XVI, pt. 1, 3, herinafter abbreviated as "Slave Narratives," Texas.
4. B. A. Botkin (ed.), **Lay My Burden Down: A Folk History of Slavery** (Chicago, 1945), 236-237.
5. Statement of William M. Adams, "Slave Narratives," Texas, XVI, pt. 1, 11; statement of Armstead Barrett, **ibid.**, 47-48; statement of Tom Holland, **ibid.**, pt. 2, 144-147; Walter Cotton, **History of Negroes of Limestone County** (Mexia, Texas, 1939), 11.
6. Statement of Sarah Ford, "Slave Narratives," Texas, XVI, pt. 2, 46.
7. Amelia Barr, **All the Days of My Life: An Autobiography** (New York, 1913), 251.
8. Allen W. Trelease, **White Terror: The Ku Klux Klan Conspiracy and Southern Reconstruction** (New York, 1971), xvii.
9. New Orleans Tribune, June 11, 17, 18 and August 5, 1865; P. F. Duggan to James Kirkman, August 1, 1867, Letters Sent, Sub-Assistant Commissioner, Columbia, Texas, Bureau of Refugees, Freedmen, and Abandoned Land, Record Group 105, National Archives, Washington, D.C., hereafter abbreviated BRFAL, RG 105, NA.
10. Houston Tri-Weekly Telegraph, October 6, 1865; William F. Fleming, "San Antonio: The History of a Military City, 1865-1880" (unpublished Ph.D. dissertation, University of Pennsylvania, 1963), 29-30; Louis Constant to Andrew J. Hamilton, October 18, 1865, Andrew J. Hamilton Governor's Correspondence, Archives, Texas State Library, Austin, Texas.
11. Statement of Jacob Branch, "Slave Narratives," Texas, XVI, Pt. 1, 142; statement of Sarah Allen, **ibid.**, statement of Joe Barnes, **ibid.**, 46; Botkin (ed.), **Lay My Burden Down**, 229; William P. Ballinger Diary, July 11, 17, 1865, William P. Ballinger Papers, Archives, University of Texas Library, Austin, Texas; for a tabular analysis of black population trends in Texas from 1850 to 1930 see Mattie Bell, "The Growth and Distribution of the Texas Population" (unpublished M. A. thesis, Baylor University, 1935), 126-136.
12. Botkin (ed.), **Lay My Burden Down**, 223.
13. Houston Tri-Weekly Telegraph, June 30, July 12, October 6, 1865; New York Times, July 17, 1865; **San Antonio Herald**, October 14, December 29, 1865; Byron Porter to A. B. Coggeshall, October 15, 1866, Letters Sent, Sub-Assistant Commissioner, Austin, Texas, BRFAL, RG 105, NA.
14. Amelia Barr to Jennie, June 3, 1865, Amelia Barr Papers, Archives, University of Texas Library.

15. Houston Tri-Weekly Telegraph, July 10, 12, 1865; Huntsville Item, July 14, 1865.
16. Flake's Daily Bulletin, September 1, 1865.
17. Statement of Minerva Bendy, "Slave Narratives," Texas, XVI, pt. 1, 68-69; statement of Armstead Barrett, ibid., 47; statement of Fred Brown, ibid., 159; statement of Sarah Ford, ibid., pt. 2, 46; statement of Eli Davison, ibid., pt. 1, 295-296.
18. Botkin (ed.), Lay My Burden Down, 247.
19. Charles E. Culver to Charles Garretson, November 1, 1867, Letters Sent, Sub-Assistant Commissioner, Cotton Gin, Texas, BRFAL, RG 105, NA.
20. Statement of Lucy Thomas, "Slave Narratives," Texas, XVI, pt. 4, 90; statement of Ella Washington, ibid., 133.
21. James McCleery to J. W. Alvord, September 7, 1869, Letters Sent, Superintendent of Education, Shreveport, Louisiana, BRFAL, RG 105, NA; **Harrison Flag** (Marshall), May 2, 1867; statement of John Love, "Slave Narratives," Texas, XVI, pt. 3, 26; Botkin (ed.), Lay My Burden Down, 76, 247.
22. Statement of Elige Davison, "Slave Narratives," Texas, XVI, pt. 1, 298.
23. Houston Tri-Weekly Telegraph, June 5, 28, 30, October 20, 1865; Flake's Daily Bulletin, August 31, 1865.
24. Balinger Dairy, May 13, 1865, Balinger Papers.
25. Barr to Jennie, October 25, 1866, Barr Papers.
26. Flake's Weekly Bulletin, November 19, 1865, February 7, 21, 1866; San Antonio Weekly Herald, August 31, 1865.
27. William L. Richter, "The Army in Texas During Reconstruction, 1865-1870" (unpublished Ph.D. dissertation, Louisiana State University, 1971), 203.
28. San Antonio Daily Herald, September 2, 1865.
29. Galveston Tri-Weekly News, October 13, August 25, 1865; Porter to Chancey Morse, February 1, 1866, Letters Sent, Sub-Assistant Commissioner, Houston, Texas, BRFAL, RG 105, NA.
30. Sallie M. Lentz, "Highlights of Early Harrison County," Southwestern Historical Quarterly, LXI (October, 1957), 254; Fleming, "San Antonio: The History of a Military City, 1865-1880," 31.
31. Galveston Tri-Weekly News, October 13, 1865; Flake's Daily Bulletin, July 29, 1865.
32. Jacob DeGress to E. M. Gregory, October 24, 1865, Letters Sent, Provost Marshall of the District of East Texas, BRFAL, RG 105, NA; U. S., House of Representatives, House Executive Documents, 39th Cong., 2d Sess., 1866 (Serial 1292), Document No. 61, 1-4.
33. B. F. Barkley to Hamilton, October 30, 1865, D. B. Lucky to Hamilton, October 16, 1865, Hamilton Governor's Correspondence; Houston Tri-Weekly Telegraph, July 17, 1865.
34. Statement of Armstead Barrett, "Slave Narratives," Texas, XVI, pt. 1, 47; statement of Tom Holland, ibid., pt. 2, 146.
35. Claude Elliott, "The Freedmen's Bureau in Texas," Southwestern Historical Quarterly, LVI (July, 1952), 6.

36. See complaint books, 1865-1868, Sub-Assistant Commissioner, Houston, Texas, BRFAL, RG 105, NA; **Galveston Tri-Weekly News,** October 13, 1865; Lenard B. Groce Dairy, December 18, 1866, January 15, 1867, Lenard B. Groce Papers, Archives, University of Texas Library.

37. U. S., House of Representatives, **House Reports,** 39th Cong., 1st Sess., 1866 (Serial 1273), Report No. 30, 46-47, 77.

38. Statement of John Bates, "Slave Narratives," Texas, XVI, pt. 1, 52; U. S., House of Representatives, **House Executive Documents,** 39th Cong., 1st Sess., 1866 (Serial 1256), Document No. 70, 146-147; **Harrison Flag,** May 2, 1867; DeGress to Provost Marshall, Millican, October 31, 1865, DeGress to Gregory, November 30, 1865, Letters Sent, Sub-Assistant Commissioner, Houston, Texas, BRFAL, RG 105, NA.

39. Statement of Anderson Edwards, "Slave Narratives," Texas, XVI, pt. 2, 8; statement of Josie Brown, ibid., pt. 1, 164; Botkin (ed.), **Lay My Burden Down,** 233; Barkley to Hamilton, October 30, 1865, Hamilton Governor's Correspondence.

40. Porter to Albert Evans, December 28, 1866, Letters Sent, Sub-Assistant Commissioner, Austin, Texas, James Oakes to Kirkman, July 31, 1867, Sub-Assistant Commissioner, Austin, Texas, BRFAL, RG 105, Na; Botkin (ed.), **Lay My Burden Down,** 76.

41. **Flake's Daily Bulletin,** December 3, 1865.

42. DeGress to Gregory, October 19, November 30, 1865, Letters Sent, Sub-Assistant Commissioner, Houston, Texas, BRFAL, RG 105, NA.

43. Statement of Susan Merritt, "Slave Narratives," Texas, XVI, pt. 3, 78.

44. **Flake's Daily Bulletin,** August 2, 1865.

45. U. S., House of Representatives, **House Reports,** 39th Cong., 1st Sess., 1866 (Serial 1273), Report No. 30, 39; U. S., Senate, **Senate Executive Documents,** 39th Cong., 1st Sess., 1866 (Serial 1238), Document No. 27, 81-86, 147-150.

46. **New Orleans Tribune,** December 16, 1865; Constant to Hamilton, October 18, 1865, Hamilton Governor's Correspondence.

47. Charles F. Rand to Kirkman, April 30, 1867, Letters Sent, Sub-Assistant Commissioner, Marshall, Texas, BRFAL, RG 105, NA.

48. Wallace, **Texas in Turmoil,** 164-169; Hamilton's Proclamation to Freedmen, November 17, 1865, Hamilton Governor's Correspondence.

49. Hiram Christian to Hamilton, October 21, 1865, Hamilton Governor's Correspondence; U. S., House of Representatives, **House Executive Documents,** vol. III, pt. 1, 40th Cong., 3rd Sess., 1868 (Serial 1367), Document No. 1, 1052; DeGress to Gregory, October 24, 1865, Letters Sent, Sub-Assistant Commissioner, Houston, Texas, BRFAL, RG 105, NA.

50. Robert W. Shook, "The Federal Military in Texas, 1865-1870," **Texas Military History,** VI (Spring, 1967), 6; **New York Times,** July 17, 1865.

51. Bell I. Wiley, "Billy Yank and the Black Folk," **Journal of Negro History**, XXXVI (January, 1951), 35-52; Porter to Gregory, January 13, 1866, Letters Sent, Sub-Assistant Commissioner, Houston, Texas, BRFAL, RG 105, NA.

52. James E. Sefton, **The United States Army and Reconstruction, 1865-1877** (Baton Rouge, 1967), 45.

53. William T. Sherman to John Sherman, February 23, 1866, in Rachel Sherman Thorndike (ed.), **The Sherman Letters** (New York, 1969), 263.

54. See Arlen L. Fowler, **The Black Infantry in the West, 1869-1891** (Westport, Connecticut, 1971), 139.

55. James D. Richardson (comp.), **Messages and Papers of the Presidents** (10 vols.; Washington, 1904), VI, 321-323.

56. Sefton, **The United States Army and Reconstruction, 1865-1877**, appendix B, 261-262; Shook, "The Federal Military in Texas, 1865-1870," 18-19.

57. Elliott, "The Freedmen's Bureau in Texas," 4, 24; Shook, "The Federal Military in Texas, 1865-1870," 22.

58. U. S., Senate **Senate Executive Documents**, 39th Cong., 2d Sess., 1867 (Serial 1276), Document No. 6, 151; U. S., House of Representatives, **House Executive Documents**, vol. III, 39th Cong., 2d Sess., 1867 (Serial 1285), Document No. 1, 721.

59. U. S. Senate, **Senate Executive Documents**, 39th Cong., 2d Sess., 1867 (Serial 1276), Document No. 6, 148-150; New York Times, February 19, 1866; C. S. Tambling to George Whipple, December 1, 1865, Texas Correspondence, American Missionary Association, Archives, Amistad Research Center, Dillard University, New Orleans, Louisiana.

10

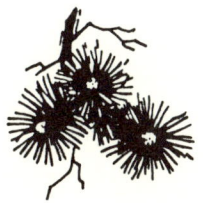

We lived in the "piney woods" of East Texas. My father had a sawmill.¹ We were a long way from any town. Eight miles was a half day's journey in those days, with deep sand and stumpy roads. There were very few roads that one could travel with a hack or buggy. In the winter we were water bound as all streams were swollen and dangerous. There were foot logs but very few bridges. We did not have schools or churches except in the small towns or thickly settled neighborhoods. We had cottage prayer meetings once in a long while.

My brothers went to school in the old town of Plantersville.² The terms were short but they had a good school. The pupils rode horseback. They took their lunches in tin buckets with tight lids. We had never met "Mr. Germ" then but he was there. The lunches consisted of biscuits, cornbread and homemade syrup. We had fresh meat and fruit of some kind. We had fine orchards and there was plenty of wild fruit. We had berries — blackberries and dewberries — wild plums and grapes as well as the cultivated fruits. The woods were full of game. My father and my brothers were great hunters and fishermen. My mother cooked anything, such as rabbits, o'possums, squirrels, turkeys, deer, wild ducks, geese, quail, and "coons" but she would not eat very many of these things and if mother wouldn't eat it I wouldn't either. We also had a few sheep, goats and Longhorn cattle. We would milk twenty cows and very seldom made more butter than we could use. Once in a while we would sell a pound. Later my father crossed the Longhorns with Durham, which was a wonderful improvement.

We always had dogs, hounds at that. We had a cur or bulldog as watch dogs. As a child I hated the hounds because they were always hungry and we could not get outside with anything to eat or they would take it away from us. Our men never thought of killing for sport but just for food. Sometimes the neighbor men would come over and bring their dogs. They would have a big fox hunt but the fox was most always safe. When I heard all those old hounds on its trail — I could tell when they struck a warm trail — I would cover up my head and hope that the fox would get away, even if they did like chickens and geese. We had a flock of geese for their feathers as everyone was expected to have a big fat feather bed in those days. Believe me, they are still fine. We also had ducks, turkeys, and peacocks. We drew the tails of the male peacock in the summer. Mother[3] nearly always received five dollars for each tail. They were made into long handled fans or brushes to fan flies off of the table while eating. These fans were very fancy and beautiful. Screens were unknown at that time. There were some good old black "mammies" who went among the neighbors every six weeks in the summer to pick geese. They could pick about thirty in a day. We also picked the ducks.

I had one sister and brother younger than I. We did not have any place to go but we were happy. We had swings, seesaws, and stick horses. My older brother would give us a dime, when he was at home, if we would not ride astride for he did not like to see little girls astride. As soon as he was gone we would straddle our horses and away we would go. We would pace, trot, and lope. We had a play house and we had dolls. We learned a little about sewing by making doll clothes.

There was a little cloud coming into our happy young lives. There was not any school near enough for us to go alone, so that was my first heartache when I had to leave mother and stay with a neighbor and go to school. But the term was short, only three months. Later I went to my brother's house in the old town of Montgomery[4] for two terms of school. That was the only real school I ever went to and I did very well. I would have done better but all I thought of was Friday when one of my brothers would come for me to spend the weekend at home. I remember one day brother Frank came for me and told me that I had better not try to go home this week as the creek was rising when he crossed it. He was afraid that he would have to swim it on the way back home. I begged him to take me anyway as I would not mind if he were with me. Old "Reb", his horse, was a big old fellow. I rode behind Frank; so when we came to the creek it was out of its banks but we went across safely. Old "Reb" went under all but his head but we hung on some way. Of course, we were like "drowned rats" but that was okay with me for we got home in a little while. When I saw my mother coming to meet me I cried because she was so glad to see me and I was so glad to see her after almost a week and I was so glad I had come.

I don't think children now get homesick like we did, for mother was all we had. We did not have many playmates or a lot of places to go and we were taught to love home. We did not have Sunday School in the country, but my mother was a wonderful mother. She would read to us out of the family Bible and tell us of the Master. She taught us to trust him and we would be saved, and "To do unto others as we would have them do unto us." Surely He was with us for we would roam through the woods looking for turkey nests and picking berries when every step we took was one of danger. I never remember being afraid of the many snakes or wild animals that were plentiful at that time. We were taught to look out for stray Negroes that would stroll through the woods. They were the "Big bad wolf" in our happy lives. There was one especially scary clump of bushes and trees we sometimes had to come through. I would take my little sister's hand and say "Jessie, let's say a prayer and then run like the dickens." We always came through unharmed.

When the Sabbath day came around we had no place to go, but we always bathed, put on our Sunday clothes, and dressed the beds up and had the house looking nice as we usually had company.

In the spring mother would take us walking in the woods and tell us of the trees and the flowers. She seemed to know the name and habit of all of them and some of them we used as medicine. I remember the Red Oak and the Sweetgum bark. We would drink water steeped in the bark whenever we had the flu or bowel trouble.[5] Then there was the Haw, both red and black, with their lovely sweet scented blooms, and the Dogwood with its beautiful blossoms almost covering the trees. They looked like a snow bank. When the Magnolias would come in bloom we would have long poles to twist off the blossoms from the highest limbs. The Locus was so sweet and beautiful too. I seem to see the old pines with the new growth in the spring. Some of them were so tall they would be fifty feet to the first limb. I wonder if sometimes my child eyes saw things more beautiful than they really were. The long veils of moss on the oaks in the spring, for instance. I have never seen moss that looked like that, with its long streamers floating in the breeze with the new growth in the spring. It was wonderful. And I must not forget the dainty little [Sumac] with its dark, glossy green foliage. It was so pretty with other flowers or wreaths. The sassafras with its ash colored foliage from which we made tea in the spring. We were all supposed to drink it once a day to cleanse the blood but I never did drink much of it.

When I was about ten years old, life changed some for us. Mother's sister came to live near us. She had a girl near my age, one grown son and another daughter; so they had parties and we learned to dance. Not like they dance now, we had . . . [the] "Virginia Reel" and a lot more square dances. Everytime we were together we always danced. My cousin played the "fiddle" for us; so we did not care whether we had a party or not, for we were always dancing.

In the old days it cost very little to travel. Anyone would take you in and make you welcome and seemed to enjoy your company. But even then it was hard on the housewife as she would have to prepare extra meals and find a place for them to sleep. When a strange man would ride up, my father would say "Light" and he would "light" and then father would say to my brother, "Put this man's horse up and feed it." Then to mother he would call, "Mother, have you a bite to eat for this stranger?" So often she would have to cook extra. I remember my father went to North Texas about some land matters and was gone about a week. He went horseback, of course. When he returned he said he only spent one dollar while he was gone and that he gave to a widow and her children for keeping him one night.

In the afternoon mother would sit on the porch with her mending basket and darn and mend. We would sit near her and listen while she would tell us of the old times when she was young and how much better times she had then. For one thing, mother had a sewing machine that you turned by hand. I believe she bought it in 1867. She also had a cook stove. We did not have to mold so many candles, either, as we had little brass lamps with round wicks. We also had matches but they were high, about 50^c for a small box about the size of a penny box now. We covered the fire with ashes and never let it go out. Sometimes a neighbor would come before daylight to get a shovel of coals to start a fire. We would have lighters made out of colored paper to light pipes or candles. In winter we used rich pine to make torches if we had to look after the chickens. The black pitch would run out of these torches and if it dropped on your hand or arm it was just too bad. But later father bought some beautiful glass lamps with chimneys, and a lantern. We thought them wonderful and fine.

Mother would make her own soap by dripping lye through grease and ashes. Of course we had an old hopper. We bought a soap we called turpentine soap. It was expensive but was fine for white ruffles, shirts, white dresses and fine linens. Our washboards were very crude, too, and Monday mornings you could hear the old battling sticks doing their duty.

Later in mother's life, father bought her a sewing machine that you peddled with your foot and that was some better. The name of it was Howe and it made about as much noise as a Model T Ford car. Later we traded the Howe for the American machine and it was almost as good as the machines are now. It had all of the attachments. There was a hemmer, tucker, gatherer, and a quilter. Mother could not get the hang of it then but I could use them from the first day. Mother was so proud of me. I would tuck, hem and gather ruffles by the yards for neighbors, and quilt bonnet tops too. Believe me, mother was not the only one that thought I was smart. I believed it myself.

There were very few places we could go those days in buggies. We had to go horseback. Ladies all had long riding skirts with large buttons down the front. Of course they had to ride side saddle. The first woman I ever heard of or saw riding astride was the great sculptress, Elizabet Ney. She and her husband, Dr. Montgomery, would go to the county seat on business. At that time Old Montgomery was the county seat. She and her husband had a large saw mill not very far from my father's mill.[6] I remember one morning she and Dr. Montgomery came to our house for the first time. Elizabet Ney had on pants and was riding astride. Our mill at the time was running full blast with a lot of buyers, visitors and a full crew of men. Father thought at the time he would have to stop the mill for fear of accidents as every one wanted to see a woman in riding pants and riding astride. She was a great artist or sculptress but her fame was nothing to the working men at the mill. Her pants and the way she rode were the attraction. If there are any of the oldtimers living they will speak of her as the woman who wore pants and rode astride. After that she came every now and then. She and Dr. Montgomery would stop at our home and ask for coffee and sometimes fresh eggs. They ate the eggs raw, just breaking them in a glass and putting salt and pepper on them. My father tried to teach my sister and me not to stare at strangers, so while they were drinking their coffee in the dining room we would go back in the kitchen where she could not see us and gaze all we wanted to. We need not have been afraid of her. We could have gone in where they were and I doubt if she would have even seen or noticed us. I never remember seeing her smile or notice the beautiful shrubs, flowers, trees, or lovely snow white turkeys, lambs, or anything that most strangers would have enjoyed. Her mind seemed to be in the clouds and, strange to say, she had a son about six or eight years old and he was still in dresses the last time I heard of him.

We children did not wear pants, but we had long pantaloons almost to the shoe tops. Our Sunday pantaloons were very fancy with silk and lace. Our dresses seemed to me to have three widths in them and were a bit longer than now. You could not see much of a little girl's legs then. We called our legs limbs and would not have thought of saying leg or limb in company. We were taught to be seen and not heard. We understood a lot too. Mother would always say that little pitchers had big ears. We were just as eager to know about life as the children are now, but the children are wiser now and can tell their grandmothers a few things that will make them sit up and take notice.

Mother did not go out much but we had three nice neighbors. Our families had been friends for years. They would come in and spend the day or afternoon sometimes and how happy we would be to have girls our ages to play with. If they came in the afternoon we would always have coffee, little cakes or biscuits, and butter. Everyone would have some kind of refreshments when old neighbors came for a visit. When I see the beautiful playgrounds of today with their merry-go-rounds, fancy swings, seesaws and swimming pools and many other things, I wonder if the children get the thrill out of them that I did when I found a goose nest full of large snow white eggs. The old mother goose would make her nest by some log and would always cover up the nest when she left it. But the old gander would always show me where the nest was. He would get on top of a log and call every now and then. If I heard him I would have no trouble in finding the nest but had plenty of trouble getting the eggs if he was still there. I never could wait for him to leave: so he would pinch my arms black and blue but I got those eggs just the same. And how I did love those geese. There is nothing any sweeter than a baby goslin so soft, helpless, and silly. Children don't seem to remember things that happen now.

 I was not quite four when my younger sister was born, but I remember her little red face as plain as yesterday. When she was three months old my oldest sister was married. She was such a sweet companion for my mother and such a help and comfort, too. It was hard for mother to give her up. The night of the wedding we had a big supper. Mother and some of the old friends cooked for days. Her dress was white Swiss with a long veil with orange blossoms. I seem to see my mother yet, the day after my sister married, when they came for her trunk, bedding, and so many pretty quilts. With tears streaming down her face she bade farewell to the first child to leave the home nest.

 My sister and her husband only lived about a mile from us. In less than two years they moved near where the town of Rogers[7] is now. The only town near them was Belton. After my brother-in-law had his farm in good shape, they had someone to care for things so they could come to see us in the summer. They came in a covered wagon and I never see one to this day that I don't think of those wonderful visits. They must have gone three years or more before they came the first time when they had a little girl with black curly hair. Her name was Florence. We called her "Babe." We thought her the prettiest and smartest girl living. Mother could not love her enough. It seems that my sister did not have any Negroes near them so the first day they came my little sister and I had "Babe" in our playhouse when in came Pete and Anna, our colored friends and playmates. I will never forget the scream Babe gave when she saw them. But by talking and petting she soon got used to them; but anyway, she told her mother to make them wash their faces! There was one Negro girl on the place who was just my age. If she could have lived now, she would rival the Mills Brothers. She sounded just like a band when she hummed or sang her songs. She made such fine dance music that we made her sing while we danced.

It seems to me now that father may have had nine or ten families on the mill yard and they were sick quite a bit and there was where my dear mother was to be found — with the sick and dying. She always helped to put away the dead. She was at every birth, too. She also helped at the weddings of some of the young folk. You could not buy a coffin nearer than Houston, so the coffins had to be made. I never hear a hammer at night that I don't think what that sound used to mean. We had a graveyard right near the mill under some big trees. Father had it fenced and I wonder if it could be found now.[8]

In 1870, the year my sister married, my sister Livinia, older than I, passed away. So poor mother had a birth, wedding and death within a few months. Until I was about fourteen my father was making money with his saw mill; then so many better improved mills were being built around us and our timber was about all used up as we only sawed the best timber. He tried to find a new location but it cost so much to move and we would have to buy a lot of new machinery, so my poor father went broke. Then trouble was as now — [it] never came alone.

In the spring my brother, Charles, was very ill with pneumonia and his life was threatened for three weeks. But he soon recovered. My mother's only sister was stricken with the same complaint. Mother had not had time to rest from nursing my brother before she had to nurse her sister, who passed away in about ten days. She left her three children without a mother or father. But my mother's brother lived with them and he was a good man. We all loved him. The children took their mother to the old Springer graveyard about eighteen miles away. It took a day to go and a day to dig the grave and put her away. Then it took a day to come home. The day they left Uncle Rie came over to eat supper with us but said he did not feel well and in a short time he had a chill. Mother took him home and stayed with him awhile. Father went for a doctor but the doctor couldn't do anything and he also passed away in 24 hours. When my cousins returned home they had to start back with Uncle Rie's remains.

In about ten days it was to be my mother's birthday, the first of March. Brother Frank came in with a large catfish so mother told me to go after her poor sister's children. I can never forget that supper for it was the last supper my mother ever cooked. Right after we were finished with supper she told one of my brothers she was cold. Father became alarmed and sent Brother Frank for Doctor Irons. He worked faithfully with her but she left us. When we returned from putting her away I was dazed. I did not know what to do. My poor little brother and sister were lost too. My father was pitiful. How were we to live without our mother? Father would not stay in mother's room. He told my sister and me that it was ours, so he took little brother Baylor and moved in a room across the hall. My happy childhood was over. I became a woman in three days. I who had never had a care took up my mother's burdens. I tried to make my father and brothers comfortable. With my young sister's help we did our best but that was not so good. I wonder why I was so selfish not to have helped mother more while she was with us. She was only fifty-four when she died.

I don't remember how long we stayed with father and my brothers. Anyway, they had to leave us alone most all day and they were anxious. They did not feel that it was safe for us to be alone, so my sister and I went to father's sister's [house] to live. Then Brother John came for Sister Jessie and my oldest sister took my brother Baylor. We knew this separation was best for us but that did not keep the hurt from our young hearts. We knew that we would never walk the same path or be together any more. I stayed on with my aunt until I married. I believe that my life in some ways was not as hard as that of my mother, although I never heard her complain. I have had many comforts that she never had. I went places, have seen more, made more mistakes than she ever made, and I have had some troubles that she never had.

Notes

Mrs. Mattie Dupree Steussy's "Memoirs" have been preserved by Mrs. L. C Hooper of Victoria, Texas, who generously contributed from her extensive notes on the Dupree family.

1. Mrs. Steussy's father was Captain Franklin Goldstein Dupree (1826-1914), one time-member of Company "H", 26 Mounted Calvary, C. S. A. Dupree's father, Colonel Lewis Dupree (1801-1855) was a veteran of the Seminole War and established a plantation in 1842 on his arrival in Texas. Lewis Dupree's migration was the result of encouragement from his cousin, Mirabeau B. Lamar. The plantation was located in what is now Grimes and Montgomery Counties and was traversed by the Old San Antonio Road connecting Montgomery and Navasota. Franklin G. Dupree owned sawmills at Hockley, Hempstead, Calvert, and Hearne. His initial efforts included adapting steam engines from the **Harriet Lane** to his mill operations. Mrs. L. C. Hooper to Robert W. Shook, August 11, 1972; H. A. Trexler, "The Harriet Lane and the Blockade of Galveston," **Southwestern Historical Quarterly,** XXV (October, 1931); Worth S. Ray, **Austin Colony Pioneers** (Austin, 1970), 92; Eighth Census of the United States (1850). Grimes County Texas, 69; **Ibid.**, (1860), 80; Charles Spurlin, "John Lewis Dupree," **Texas Bar Journal,** 30 (December, 1967). Duprees appear in numerous nineteenth-century Texas newspapers. Surname Index, Newspaper Collection, University of Texas Archives, Austin.

2. Plantersville is located in southeast Grimes County. The **Handbook of Texas,** edited by Walter P. Webb (Austin, 1952), II 384-385; Eric L. Blair, **Early History of Grimes County,** (n.p.), 1930.

3. Canzadia Tines Springer Dupree (1830-1882) was Franklin G. Dupree's first wife. She descended from Zacariah Landrum (1776-1833), Revolutionary War veteran and one of "Austin's 300" who arrived in Texas in 1831. His wife was Letita Tines (Tynes) (1776-1848).

4. Montgomery was designated the county seat of Montgomery County in 1837. Both Montgomery and Plantersville were on the Gulf, Colorado, and Sante Fe Railroad. The county seat was moved to Conroe in 1871. **Handbook,** II, 226. For details on development in the area see W. H. Gandy, "A History of Montgomery County, Texas," (unpublished Master of Arts thesis, University of Houston, 1952).

5. William R. Hogan discusses early Texian cures in **The Texas Republic** (Norman, 1947). Numerous guides to medicinal herbs were available, judging by old family libraries, to late nineteenth cen-

tury Texans. Dr. R. V. Pierce's, **The Peoples Common Sense Medical Advisor** (Buffalo, 1875) was a popular volume and contained a full chapter on homemade remedies.

    6. Elisabet Ney and Dr. Montgomery were without peers as early members of the state's artistic and philosophic community. Their lives are recreated in numerous sources: **Handbook, II, 55-56, 278;** Vernon Loggins, "Elisabet Ney at Liendo Plantation," **Southwest Review,** (Autumn, 1946); Vernon Loggins, **Two Romantics and their Ideal Life; Elisabet Ney, Sculptor** (New York, 1916); Morris T. Keeton, **The Philosophy of Edmund Montgomery** (Dallas, 1950); I. K. Stephens, **The Hermit Philosopher of Liendo** (Dallas, 1951); Frank Edd White, "A History of the Territory That Now Constitutes Waller County, Texas, from 1821 to 1884" (unpublished Master of Arts thesis, University of Texas, Austin, 1936).

    7. Rogers, Texas, is located near Temple and Belton. The community was established in 1881 and after a boom during World War I began a decline. **Handbook, II, 144, 499.**

    8. The Dupree Cemetery has been rescued from the wilderness near Navasota.

11

Margie E. Neal: First Woman Senator in Texas

by
Walter L. Harris

Walter L. Harris is a former teacher of history at Lon Morris College, where he also served as Business Manager. He is Administrative Assistant to the Superintendent of the Jacksonville, Texas district.

11

When Senator Margie E. Neal first invaded the masculine sanctity of the Texas Senate in January, 1927, she had already amassed a series of honors and "firsts" in public life which would have been sufficient to secure for her a place of prominence in the history of East Texas.

Born near Clayton in Panola County in 1875, she was the daughter of William Lafayette Neal and Martha Ann Gholston Neal, both of whom came to Texas from Georgia. The desire of her parents to provide their children with good educational opportunities prompted a move from the country home near Clayton to the county seat town of Carthage in 1884.[1]

Miss Neal's first contact with high political officials came about 1885 or 1886 when Governor John Ireland came to Carthage for a speaking engagement. She recalled many years later that the impression made on her young mind by the appearance of a governor was profound.[2]

In the fall of 1891 she enrolled in the Panola County Male and Female College in Carthage, the first high school established in Panola County. Within a year she received a scholarship to Sam Houston Normal Institute at Huntsville. In the spring of 1893 she earned a first grade certificate, and by fall she began her teaching career in the Mount Zion community in Eastern Panola County.[3] During the academic year 1894-1895 Miss Neal returned to Sam Houston, and although she had intended to complete the requirements for graduation, circumstances were such that she never returned to school after 1895.

For several years she taught in various school systems including Forney, Scottsville in Harrison County, Marlin, and Fort Worth. While in Marlin Miss Neal became acquainted with a young Falls County attorney named Tom Connally.[4]

In 1904 Margie was forced to return to Carthage because of the failing health of her mother. The return to Carthage was related in part to the opportunity to purchase a weekly newspaper, **The Texas Mule**, which Miss Neal published for eight and one-half years.[5] She did, however, change the name of the paper to **The East Texas Register**, which she considered to be more appropriate to her personality. She thus became one of the first women newspaper publishers in the state and won wide acclaim for her progressive approach to community, state, and national problems. She was a progressive editor in a progressive era and was highly successful in the newspaper business.

In 1912 the condition of her mother had deteriorated so much that she was forced to retire from publishing and to devote most of her time to the care of her mother.[7] As a private citizen she continued to experience a deep desire to serve her community and to promote civic betterment. By 1916, Miss Neal had become once more active in community and regional affairs.[8] The valuable part women played in war work, combined with their influence on a special session of the legislature in 1918, gained for them the right to vote in Texas primary elections. Miss Neal was secretary of the Panola County

Equal Suffrage Association and, not surprisingly, became the first woman to register as a voter in Panola County.[9] In the same year she was to become the first woman member of the State Democratic Executive Committee.[10] In 1920 Miss Neal was a delegate to the Democratic National Convention which met in San Francisco.

Her activities were curtailed briefly in 1920 by the death of her mother but by the spring of 1921 she had become involved in a task which for the next six years was to occupy a major part of her time.[12] Governor Pat Neff appointed her as the first woman member of the State Normal School Board of Regents — and once again Margie E. Neal was in close contact with Texas education. She could have hardly been more happy. During the 1920's she remained active in Democratic Party affairs, but her major energies were concentrated in the area of education. As a member of the Board of Regents she was instrumental in the selection of Nacogdoches as the site for a new college and in the selection of A. W. Birdwell of San Marcos as president of Stephen F. Austin State Normal College.[13] It was largely her work as a regent that prompted her decision to run for the Senate. She came to the conclusion that she might do more for education with a vote on the floor of the House or Senate than as a regent sitting in the gallery. In March, 1926 she announced as a candidate for the Texas Senate from the second senatorial district.[14]

Her platform espoused four major goals: first, there was the need for better schools — especially rural schools — which was to be met through an increased per capita apportionment for scholastics; second, there was a pressing demand for an improved system of highways which she proposed to meet through a new gasoline tax; the third goal which was never explained precisely involved the encouragement and aiding of farmers, labor, and capital in Texas; finally there was a demand for fewer and better laws and for improved law enforcement.[15]

The campaign was clean, strenuous, and rewarding. Her only opponent was Gary B. Sanford of Shelby County, and Miss Neal carried four of the five counties in the district, trailing her opponent only in his home county.[16]

An acquaintance and friend of Miss Neal during her days as a senator, Mrs. Oveta Culp Hobby, described her in a 1952 tribute as follows:

> In the Senate Miss Margie was a unique figure: First, simply because she was a woman; and second, because she was so unlike those driving, militant, admirable women — but not always enchanting women — that we were left to expect after the suffragettes had made their march in the United States. Miss Margie felt as free to be feminine as a Senator as she had as a private citizen of Carthage.[17]

In the Fortieth Legislature she served as chairman of the Committee on Privileges and Elections and of the Committee on Rules, but her greatest joy and most outstanding service probably came through her role on the Senate committee on Educational Affairs.[18] She worked diligently, though not always successfully, for higher standards in teacher certification.

Senator Neal was generally sympathetic with the legislative program of Governor Dan Moody and she certainly shared his sincere aspirations for reform and good government. She was particularly interested in the matter of prison reform and was a member of a legislative inspection party which visited several prison farms in South Texas in February, 1927.[19]

It was legislation regarding education, however, which made Miss Neal most conspicuous during the Fortieth Legislature. She was conversant both with the problems of public shcools and higher educational institutions, having had some experience with each. Her legislative contributions to the field of education fell largely into three major categories: matters relating to educational standards, matters relating to efficient educational administration, and matters relating to curriculum content.

Shortly after the session opened Senator Neal introduced the measure which first cast upon her the spotlight of statewide publicity.[20] Her years in the classroom, her experience as an editor and as a private citizen of

Carthage, together with her close contact with teacher training institutions during the 1920's had made Miss Neal an ardent champion of high standards for Texas education. In the Thirty-ninth Legislature Senator I. D. Fairchild, of Lufkin, introduced and secured the passage of a teacher certification bill which in part provided that,

> . . . Any person who for six years or more has been the holder of a state first grade certificate or its equivalent and who can furnish evidence of successful experience in teaching in the public schools for six or more sessions subsequent to September 1, 1910, shall be entitled to receive a State permanent first grade certificate.[21]

To Margie Neal such a provision was abominable, and a severe setback for quality education in Texas. Her first major bill as a senator, therefore, was directed toward the repeal of the above-quoted section of the Fairchild law. The bill was reported favorably from the Committee on Educational Affairs, and by early February it was before the Senate for consideration. On second reading Senator Thomas B. Love, of Dallas, offered and secured an amendment designed to entitle any individual to a certificate provided he had taught ". . . six or more successive years immediately preceding the issuance thereof . . . ."[22] Thus Senator Neal's bill, after being subjected to the Love amendment, was virtually no different from the Fairchild law which it was designated to repeal. The lady senator was extremely disturbed, and because of her displeasure she voted against her bill on its final passage.

The next day various newspapers told in a humorous vein of how Margie Neal had become so overwhelmed by parliamentary complexities that she had voted against her own bill.[23] Her reaction to the handling of this incident by the press was one of complete amazement. It was quite correct that she had voted against her own bill, but her vote was in no way elicited by parliamentary complexities. After reading the newspapers Senator Neal rose to a point of personal privilege and explained that she had voted against the amended bill because the amendment mutilated her bill so thoroughly that she no longer considered it her own. She acknowledged a certain unfamiliarity with parliamentary technicalities, and requested the continued patience and forbearance of her colleagues. She stated emphatically, however, that she desired no quarter from the gentlemen merely because she was a woman. The manner in which she spoke drew the spontaneous applause of fellow senators, and possibly went far toward making her acceptance by the Senate a reality.[24]

The teacher certification bill was lost, but complete victory could have hardly been more glorious for the sponsor. Margie Neal so conducted herself that she achieved triumph in defeat and had demonstrated unmistakably that she was the friend of high standards in Texas education. Throughout the coming months she gave to the cause of educational progress her most vigorous support.

Her experience as a regent of the State Teachers Colleges had convinced her that, generally, the best interests of the state were not served when boards of regents came from the immediate localities of the institutions they governed. She attempted to incorporate a provision reflecting this thinking into a bill increasing the number of regents for the College of Industrial Arts, but the Senate was hostile to the provision probably because such an amendment, if effected, would have opened the door to an eventual exclusion of local regents for such schools as Texas Agricultural and Mechanical College and The University of Texas — a situation the wisdom of which few senators were willing to concede.[25]

This same regent bill occasioned a revelation which gave striking emphasis to Margie E. Neal's views toward the role which women should play in government. It was held by some that since the College of Industrial Arts was a women's institution, a majority of its regents should be women. To such a view Senator Neal could not subscribe. She was not one to seek preferential treatment either for herself or for her sex and she expressed emphatic opposition to the proposal. "Miss Neal," the **Dallas News** wrote editorially, feels that "real equality is better served by letting fitness for the place have as large an influence in the choice of Regents as is possible."[26]

Another evidence of Miss Neal's concern for education was given by her perseverence in behalf of a bill making physical training a required part of the curriculum of Texas public schools. The measure provoked stubborn opposition from a group of legislators led by Senator Thomas G. Pollard, of Tyler, but Senator Neal was able, finally, to secure its passage by the Senate.[27]

One of the most creditable accomplishments of the Fortieth Legislature came in the special session of June, 1927, with the appropriation of $1,600,000 for each of the next two scholastic years,

> ... for the purpose of promoting the public school interests of rural schools and equalizing the educational opportunities afforded by the state to all children of scholastic age living in small and financially weak school districts...[28]

This was the largest rural aid appropriation in the history of Texas; and the increase, for which Senator Neal worked diligently, gave a needed boost to the quality of Texas rural education.[29]

The work of the Fortieth Legislature was completed by early in the summer of 1927, whereupon Miss Neal returned to Carthage to remain there during the legislative interim. She was much in demand as a public speaker,[30] but a substantial part of her time was spent in consulting with her constituents, in planning legislative proposals, and in mapping strategy for future sessions.[31]

Senator Neal was an alternate delegate-at-large to the Democratic National Convention of 1928 which met in Houston. Miss Neal, like many Texans, was active in her opposition to the nomination of Governor Alfred E. Smith, but unlike most of the Texas electorate she did support his candidacy for the Presidency once he became the party's nominee.[32]

The regular session of the Forty-first Legislature opened on January 8, 1929 and Governor Moody presented to the legislature a comprehensive legislative program far broader in scope than his original proposals of 1927. In the Forty-first Legislature Miss Neal became

Chairman of the Committee on Educational Affairs and was thus placed in a strategic position for service of educational interests. Soon after the regular session began, however, Senator Neal became ill and was forced to return to Carthage where she remained throughout the session.[33]

The best work of the Forty-first Legislature was done in five special sessions — all of which Senator Neal did attend. In these sessions she continued to evidence a major interest in educational affairs.

The Texas electorate in November, 1928, had adopted a constitutional amendment to provide for a State Board of Education which was to have general supervisory responsibilities over the Texas public school system. Many of the details concerning organization of the Board were left to legislative discretion and it was the hope of the governor that the legislature would promptly vitalize the amendment. The regular session was perhaps negligent in this respect and Senator Neal was determined that the first called session of the legislature should compensate for this negligence.[34]

After efforts to fight off many crippling amendments the measure finally became law and it stood as one of the really outstanding monuments to Margie E. Neal's legislative career. The law provided for a board of nine members and was widely proclaimed as the most progressive step in the history of Texas education.[35] The law remained in effect until the enactment of the far-reaching Gilmer-Aikin reforms of 1949. Board members were appointed by the governor for terms of six years. Among the duties of the state board were supervision of the apportionment of state school funds to local districts, appointment of the State Textbook Committee, investment responsibilities for the permenent school fund, and prescription of standards for the certification of teachers.[36]

One educational measure which Senator Neal championed concerned the teaching of the state and federal constitutions in the public schools of Texas. The law as finally passed provided that each high school and each college supported by public funds must offer courses in the constitutions of the United States and of Texas, and that such courses must be required for graduation.[37]

Another worthy aspect of Miss Neal's tenure as a senator concerned her interest in rehabilitation of Texas cripples. In the first called session of the Forty-first Legislature she introduced and guided to passage a measure accepting the benefits of a federal law designed to promote vocational rehabilitation of cripples.[38]

Although Senator Neal worked earnestly for the governor's program in the Moody administration, her support was not given blindly. It resulted largely from her agreement with the wisdom of Moody's basic proposals. She stood for the independence of the legislator and her relations with Moody's successor prove conclusively her aversion to unquestioning obedience to gubernatorial leadership.

In February, 1930, Senator Neal announced her candidacy for re-election to the Senate.[39] She was nominated and elected without opposition, but her second term was to be served in a period of uncommon political turbulence.

The 1930 gubernatorial contest resulted in the election of Highway Commissioner Ross Sterling. The Sterling administration was characterized by unprecedented emergency. The severity of the depression was becoming increasingly evident and economic disaster affected the lives of more and more Texans. Senator Neal's relationship with Governor Sterling was somewhat more distant than that which she had enjoyed with Governor Moody.

The year 1936 marked the one hundredth anniversary of Texas independence. For many years there had been talk of holding some type of state-wide celebration to commemorate that event, but not until 1931 did the centennial movement begin to become a really positive force. In that year Senator Neal introduced a joint resolution proposing a state constitutional amendment ". . . to authorize a Texas Centennial, commemorating the heroic period of early Texas history, and to celebrate a century of independence and progress . . . ."[40] The legislature passed the resolution, and in November, 1932, the electorate accepted the proposed amendment.[41]

Senator Neal was one of twenty-one members of the Centennial Committee, and during the period 1931 to 1934 she devoted much of her time to its work.[42]

The dearth of state income created by the constant falling of state tax payments made legislators particularly conscious of sources of revenue. Governor Sterling asked the legislature, in a 1931 special session, to pass legislation enabling the state to lease for oil exploration its lands in the bed of the Sabine River. It was estimated that about one thousand acres of the river bed lay in proven territory in the East Texas oil field, and that the state could realize millions of dollars from this property if some arrangements could be made to permit drilling in the river bed itself. Sterling argued that resources belonging to the state were being depleted without the state's realizing one cent.[43]

At the request of the Governor legislators friendly to his plan introduced legislation calculated to allow leasing and drilling of state lands in the river bed.[44] Practically all of the territory affected by this legislation lay within Senator Neal's district and her concern for the welfare of her constituents was quick to find expression. Much of the water supply for the City of Longview came from the Sabine River, and Miss Neal feared that riverbed drilling would be accompanied by tremendous pollution of the stream. Most of the legislature, however, appeared highly in favor of river-bed drilling and Senator Neal's chances to gain votes on such a heated issue were limited. The only hope for defeat of the river-bed bill lay in the clever exploitation of parliamentary technicalities.[45]

Final adjournment of the called session was set for the evening of September 29, 1931. Yet as late as the afternoon of September 28, the Senate had taken no final vote on the river-bed bill. Toward mid-afternoon Miss Neal took the floor to speak against the measure. She had hardly begun when she realized that should she hold the Senate floor until six o'clock she could prevent a final vote on the bill. The rules of the Senate provided that no bill could receive final vote within twenty-four hours of sine die adjournment, unless so ordered by a two-thirds vote of the chamber.

Although Senator Neal achieved a victory of sorts with her successful filibuster, it was short-lived in that Sterling threatened to call the legislature back into special session if it did not rescind its plans for sine die adjournment.The legislature succumbed to the threat which virtually assured passage of the river-bed bill.[46]

Seldom had Senator Neal's efforts been prompted by deeper conviction than in the river-bed struggle; yet at no time during her public career did the press react so unfavorably to her behavior. Although she was loudly acclaimed by constituents in the Longview area, her efforts were viewed with disgust by several of the state's larger newspapers.[47]

The role of Margie E. Neal as a legislator was overshadowed during much of 1932 by her participation in other political activities. Senator Neal was a delegate to the Democratic National Convention of 1932 which met in Chicago. In early September it was announced that Senator Neal would serve with Roy Miller of Corpus Christi as co-director of the Texas Roosevelt-Garner campaign.[48] There was little doubt that the Democratic party would carry the state by a comfortable majority; the goal of the campaign directors, therefore, was to make that majority the largest in the history of the state.[49]

The same spirit of unrest which denied to Herbert Hoover a second term as president proved fatal to the efforts of Governor Sterling to secure his own re-election in 1932. The Fergusons, sensing opportunity, entered Mrs. Miriam A. Ferguson as a candidate in the Democratic primary and in January, 1933 she was inaugurated as Governor of Texas for a second time.

The relationship which existed between Senator Neal and the Fergusons during the Forty-third Legislature was surprisingly good. Although she never viewed the Ferguson cause with much enthusiasm she was usually successful in avoiding open and publicized conflicts with the Ferguson elements of Texas politics. There were certainly no conflicts which compared in bitterness to incidents such as the river-bed controversy with Governor Sterling. Senator Neal supported Mrs. Ferguson on the issuance of the so-called "bread bonds" for the relief of the unemployed.[50]

By the spring of 1933 Miss Neal had decided that she would not seek a third term in the Texas Senate. Her financial situation was such that she felt she needed to find a more remunerative position.[51] She had been a leading force in the Roosevelt-Garner campaign of 1932, and was considered to be in line for an appropriate federal appointment. Since her term in the Senate did not end until January, 1935 and since the Roosevelt administration took office in March, 1933 she was frustrated by the necessity of either deserting her constituents by her resignation or seeing many of the better potential appointments made prior to her own availability for them.[52]

Early in 1934 the Forty-third Legislature met in its second and what promised to be its final special session. At the request of Senator Tom Connally Miss Neal went to Washington in April, 1934 for a conference with General Hugh Johnson, Chief of the National Industrial Recovery Administration. It appeared that the Recovery Administration would shortly have a suitable appointment for Miss Neal, and Senator Connally insisted that she begin planning toward accepting the position should it prove desirable. She assumed her Washington employment on May 15, 1934.[53] She anticipated no further special session for the issuance of more "bread bonds." Senator Neal obtained from the National Recovery Administration a leave of absence without pay in order to return to Austin for the session. Miss Neal wrote in explaining the matter to Congressman Morgan Sanders, "that my duty was here (in Austin); that the people of my district would be fully justified in saying I had left them in the lurch at the end, had I not come."[54]

After a period of Federal Service which ended in December, 1944 Miss Neal returned to her home in Carthage where she was a powerful force in community affairs for more than a quarter of a century. She died in Carthage on December 19, 1971.

Notes

1. Signed statement of Margie E. Neal, at Carthage, Texas, September 3, 1953, in Archives, Eugene C. Barker Texas History Center, The University of Texas at Austin.
2. Signed statement of Margie E. Neal at Carthage, Texas, September 4, 1953, in Archives, Eugene C. Barker Texas History Center, The University of Texas at Austin.
3. Ibid. Carthage Circulating Book Club, History of Panola County, 29; Treasurer's Annual Statement to the Commissioners Court of School Funds of the County of Panola for the Year Commencing September 1, 1893 and Ending August 31, 1894.
4. Signed statement of Margie E. Neal at Carthage, Texas, September 4, 1953, in Archives, Eugene C. Barker Texas History Center, The University of Texas at Austin.
5. Signed statement of Margie E. Neal at Carthage, Texas, November 29, 1952, in Archives, Eugene C. Barker History Center, The University of Texas at Austin.
6. East Texas Register, (Carthage) January 5, 1904.
7. East Texas Register, April 19, 1912.
8. Signed statement of Margie E. Neal at Carthage, Texas, September 9, 1953 in Archives, Eugene C. Barker Texas History Center, The University of Texas at Austin.
9. East Texas Register, March 29, June 7, June 14, June 28, and July 5, 1918.
10. Signed statement of Margie E. Neal at Carthage, Texas, September 9, 1953, in Archives, Eugene C. Barker Texas History Center, The University of Texas at Austin.
11. Ibid. Dallas Morning News, July 1, 1920.
12. Signed statement of Margie E. Neal at Carthage, Texas, September 9, 1953, in Archives, Eugene C. Barker Texas History Center, The University of Texas at Austin.
13. Minutes of State Normal School Board of Regents, 387.
14. Signed statement of Margie E. Neal, at Carthage, Texas, September 9, 1953, in Archives, Eugene C. Barker Texas History Center, The University of Texas at Austin, Panola Watchman, (Carthage) March 3, 1926.
15. Panola Watchman, July 21, 1926.
16. Panola Watchman, July 28, 1926.
17. From a tape recording of the address of Mrs. Oveta Culp Hobby at the Margie E. Neal Appreciation Day program, at Carthage, Texas, June 16, 1952, in Archives, Eugene C. Barker Texas History Center, The University of Texas at Austin.
18. Senate Journal, 40th Legislature, regular session, 4; Houston Post-Dispatch, January 21, 1927.
19. Houston Chronicle, February 27, 1927; General and Special Laws of the State of Texas, 40th Legislature, regular session, 56-57, 115-116, 228-231.

197

20. Senate Journal, 40th Legislature, regular session, 84.
21. Ibid., 39th Legislature, regular session, 182; General Laws, 39th Legislature, regular session, 449.
22. Senate Journal, 40th Legislature, regular session, 239-240. Emphasis supplied.
23. Austin American. February 8, 1927; Dallas Morning News, February 8, 1927.
24. Austin American, February 9, 1927; Dallas Morning News, February 9, 1927.
25. Senate Journal, 40th Legislature, regular session, 450; Austin American, February 21, 1927.
26. Dallas Morning News, January 29, 1927.
27. Ibid., March 2, 1927; Senate Journal, 40th Legislature, regular session, 566.
28. General and Special Laws, 40th Legislature, 1st called session, 105.
29. Senate Journal, 40th Legislature, 1st called session, 109-110; Ralph W. Steen, in Frank Carter Adams (ed.), Texas Democracy, I, 452.
30. Dallas League of Women Voters (by Mrs. Charles S. Hopkins) to Margie E. Neal, October 7, 1927; Business and Professional Women's Club of Dallas (by Mary Price) to Margie E. Neal, October 8, 1927, in personal files of Margie E. Neal, at Carthage, Texas.
31. Signed statement of Margie E. Neal, at Carthage, Texas, September 9, 1953, in Archives, Eugene C. Barker Texas History Center, The University of Texas at Austin.
32. Houston Post-Dispatch, June 24 and June 29, 1928; signed statement of Margie E. Neal, at Carthage, Texas, September 10, 1953, in Archives Eugene C. Barker Texas History Center, The University of Texas at Austin.
33. Senate Journal, 41st Legislature, regular session, 1; Dallas Morning News, January 10, 1929; Margie E. Neal to Mrs. W. R. Potter, January 17, 1929, in personal files of Margie E. Neal at Carthage, Texas.
34. General and Special Laws, 41st Legislature, regular session, 2; Dallas Morning News, January 10, and March 15, 1929.
35. Dallas Morning News, May 10, 1929.
36. General and Special Laws, 41st Legislature, 1st called session, 86-90.
37. General Laws, 41st Legislature, 2nd called session 164-165; Senate Journal, 41st Legislature, 2nd called session, 411.
38. Signed statement of Margie E. Neal, at Carthage, Texas, September 20, 1953, in Archives, Eugene C. Barker Texas History Center, The University of Texas at Austin.
39. Margie E. Neal to L. M. Nelson, February 27, 1930, in personal files of Margie E. Neal, at Carthage, Texas.
40. Senate Journal, 42nd Legislature, regular session, 692.
41. General Laws, 43rd Legislature, regular session, xx.

42. Jesse H. Jones to Margie E. Neal, July 31, 1931, in personal files of Margie E. Neal at Carthage, Texas; Jane Y. McCollum to Margie E. Neal, December 12, 1931 and December 18, 1931.

43. *Austin American*, September 24, 1931.

44. Ibid.; 42nd Legislature, 2nd called session, 107.

45. Senate Journal, 42nd Legislature, 2nd called session, 235-237; *Dallas Morning News*, September 29, 1931.

46. General and Special laws, 42nd Legislature, 2nd called session, 64-68.

47. J. W. Dalston to Margie E. Neal, September 29, 1931, in personal files of Margie E. Neal at Carthage, Texas; *Houston Post-Dispatch*, October 1, 1931.

48. *Austin American-Statesman*, September 11, 1932.

49. *Dallas Morning News*, September 28, 1932; *Marshall News Messenger*, October 2, 1932; *Austin American*, November 9, 1932.

50. General and Special Laws, 44th Legislature, regular session, xxv-xxvi, Senate Journal, 43rd Legislature, 1st called session, 274; General and Special Laws, 43rd Legislature, 1st called session, 118-131; Senate Journal, 43rd Legislature, 2nd called session, 83; General and Special Laws, 43rd Legislature, 2nd called session 31-41; Senate Journal, 43rd Legislature, 3rd called session, 254; General and Special Laws, 43rd Legislature, 3rd called session, 59-74.

51. Margie E. Neal to Nellie T. Ross, April 8, 1933, in personal files of Margie E. Neal, at Carthage, Texas.

52. Margie E. Neal to Tom Connally, February 4, 1933, in personal files of Margie E. Neal at Carthage, Texas; signed statement of Margie E. Neal at Carthage, Texas, July 30, 1954, in Archives, Eugene C. Barker Texas History Center, The University of Texas at Austin.

53. Margie E. Neal to R. E. Thomason, April 5, 1934; Margie E. Neal to Mrs. C. C. Rumsey, April 28, 1934, in personal file of Margie E. Neal at Carthage, Texas; signed statement of Margie E. Neal at Carthage, Texas, July 30, 1954, in Archives, Eugene C. Barker Texas History Center, The University of Texas at Austin.

54. Margie E. Neal to Morgan G. Sanders, September 4, 1934, in personal files of Margie E. Neal at Carthage, Texas.

12

Bride of the Forest

by
Ava Bush

Ava Bush has taught in the public schools of East Texas and in the Department of Home Economics at Stephen F. Austin State University. She is presently serving as a Dietary Consultant.

12

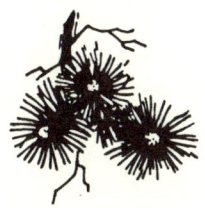

When one moves from an arid area to East Texas he is immediately impressed by the trees, usually the pines, but sometimes by another less dominant species.

In 1912, T. J. Lewis moved with his wife and several children from Runge, located between San Antonio and Goliad in Karnes County, to Elkhart. Mr. Lewis had originally come to Texas from Alabama. He was inspired by the abundance of dogwood to compose a clever riddle devised for the enjoyment of his children. To the knowledge of the writer it has never been published.

One winter evening, after the stock had been fed and the family sat around the fire for the usual Bible reading and storytelling, Mr. Lewis surprised his children with this rhyming riddle which he composed:

> One dogwood (would) bark,
> One dogwood knot (not),
> They both lay snug

> In the corner of the lot.
> A man went to see
> And they both were dead;
> They had no tail,
> And they had no head.

What a mysterious message Mr. Lewis had conjured from his observation of the native tree which grew everywhere in Anderson County — so plentiful that it was felled occasionally for firewood, though the primary household use at that time employed the small sturdy branches. They were bound together into a yard broom, familiarly referred to as a "Bresh (brush) broom," used to sweep clean the grassless area surrounding the dwelling. Of all the available shrubs, it proved most efficient (due to its nature of growth) and was long lasting.

The forest came up to the back door for many in East Texas during the early nineteen hundreds, and like Mr. Lewis, many a man looked into the time-worn face of a good wife and, against a background of spring dogwood blossoms, saw her again as his bonny young bride.

Although the dogwood of this locality **(Cornus florida)** is but one of about forty species in the temperate regions of the northern hemisphere, it is the showiest member of the genus. It is found from Massachusetts to Florida, and ranges from Ontario to Eastern and Southern Mexico. The common name is derived from the former use, in England, of a decoction of the bark of a European species, the blood-twig **(Cornus sanquinea)**, to wash mangy dogs.

The flowering dogwood is known by many other names: dog tree, false box, Florida cornel, Indian arrowwood, boxwood, bitter redberry, cornel, and various Indian names. Mon-ha-can-ni-min-schi and Hat-ta-wa-no-min-sche are recorded, as well as the shorter term **has-ki-la** used by the Alabamas and **do** used by the Koasati.

About the middle of March the dogwood blossoms. Each unit is a cluster of small greenish flowers surrounded by four large white floral bracts which are leaf-like structures with the appearance of petals. These conspicious bracts are about two and a half inches across. They are especially prominent because they appear before the leaves. Only occasionally are they pink; however, plant breeders have developed a deep rose or red dogwood that has proved extremely popular as an ornamental plant.

The true flowers develop into small, single stones having two parts. The cherry-like fruit, or drupes, color in September. These bright so-called berries, which are from one-fourth to one-half inch long, combine with the matching autumn foliage to add tremendous red beauty to the landscape. The leaves are simple, opposite the flowers, dark green above and whitish beneath.

Because legends lie in safe territory that can never be touched by scientific investigation, they seem to be legion. The legend of the dogwood is well known and has become part of the folk-lore of East Texas. Imaginative minds have woven the story of the crucifixion into the physical structure of many plants. The dogwood shows a brownish, scarred appearance at the outer edge of its notched bracts which are arranged at right angles to each other, forming a cross. Since this plant is classed as a shrub or small tree, usually only ten to fifteen feet high, legend has it that it was once a large tree, used as timbers from which Christ's cross was constructed. Afterward, its growth diminished so that it could never be forced into such service again. Its dwarfed size still tells the story, as well as the nail-scarred signs on the snow white flower crosses.

Few realize the significance of our native plants in local culture. Almost every growing herb and tree has been investigated for its ability to satisfy physiological and psychological needs. Only natural drugs were available until relatively recent times. Of their valuable uses known today, almost all were tested, established, and passed on to us by native American Indians.

Medicinal use of the dogwood by the Indians was widespread. The Alabamas, whose descendents still reside on the reservation near Livingston, Texas, drank a preparation made by boiling the inner bark in water as a treatment for dysentery. They also made a strong tea by boiling the leaves. A quart bottle full of this was poured down a horse's nostrils to relieve colic.

East Texans, as well as early explorers in the United States, used a decoction prepared of the dry bark in place of Quinine in the treatment of intermittent fevers. The bark of all parts was reputed to contain the same substance as is found in cinchona, but in different proportions. The principle is extractable with either water or alcohol. A simple infusion was often made with a teaspoonful of dried bark, or dried root bark, to a cup of boiling water. Dosage consisted of half a cupful, hot or cold, taken upon rising. It was known that the curative alkaloid was less effective than quinine and that it did not exist in appreciable quantities; however, it was thought that fevers could sometimes be warded off by merely chewing the twigs. Dogwood bark was the most common quinine substitute used during the Civil War. The bark of cherry and willow trees was also used in the same manner as the dogwood, yet sometimes the bark of all three was boiled together. The extract was usually combined with whiskey, when it was available.

Besides serving as a febrifuge, other pioneer medicines included the use of the bark infusion for sore mouth and as a poultice in external inflammations. Both of these treatments were based on tissue shrinkage due to the bark's astringent qualities.

As a dentrifice, the powdered bark was used to whiten the teeth. Some used the fresh peeled twigs for the same purpose. The Indians thought the sap of the twigs had the additional merit of preserving the gums.

In 1836, the bitter principle was separated from dogwood, and termed "cornin (or cornic acid)." In 1928, this substance was obtained in the pure state and its glycosidal nature established. Finally, in 1936, betulic acid was found in the bark of **Cornus florida**.

Although the dried bark rated as a bitter tonic, astringent, febrifuge, and antiperiodic, it was discarded from the U. S. Pharmacoposia over seventy-five years ago because its curative ingredient was judged to be only "a feeble, astringent bitter."

According to the well-known hortaculturist Liberty Hyde Bailey, the bark of the roots yields a scarlet dye, and when mixed with sulfate of iron, makes a good black ink.

The value of the wood is not debatable. It is very hard and heavy, with a fine lustrous, close grain. Only the wear-resistant sapwood is used for shuttles for cotton mills, for bobbins, tool handles, golf club heads, wedges, cogs, mauls, and engravers blocks. Dogwood is listed among the native wood that was used for carving during the Civil War. Furthermore, its grain and color make it ideal for ornamental cabinet work.

Poverty often turned the bride of the field or forest into a sober matron who was not the seeker of pleasures but, as always, the children came in for entertainment no matter how frugal the times. They found that the dogwood berries, which could be gathered as they trudged through the woods to school, were the right size and perfect ammunition for popguns designed from "switchcane" bamboo.

Because of its multiple uses, it is remarkable that the dogwood is still with us. True, it is protected by law from the roadside admirers who would break its flowering branches, unaware that its beauty is short-lived due to quick wilting. Also, many are disappointed to find that fragrance plays little part in its allure. Garden Clubs keep it on the list of plants for conservation and protect it by prohibiting its use in arrangements for flower show awards.

The dogwood is honored in several annual celebrations connected with nature trails, and historical pageants. The Tyler County Dogwood Festival had its birth in 1938 when citizens met in the interest of constructing present U. S. Highway 190. At that time the dogwoods were in bloom and it was felt that other people should be given an opportunity to enjoy their beauty in springtime. Their first festival was presented on April 6, 1940, under the auspices of the Tyler County Chamber of Commerce, and has continued annually since that time, with the fixed beginning date as the last Saturday in March. The historical pageant and queen's coronation is usually held on the first Saturday in April, at the amphitheatre in Woodville. In 1970 over thirty-five hundred people were in attendance. A parade presenting duchesses from forty surrounding towns, as well as colorful dances in the evening, highlight the occasion.

Palestine and Anderson County celebrate an annual "Dogwood Trail and Spring Tour" in late March or early April. The Texas Dogwood Trails Association, founded in 1938, helps to promote the planting program in Davey Dogwood Park. Historic homes and Old Pilgrim Church (near Elkhart), may be toured at this time.

Despite continued interest in these local festivities, the pity of the fact is that not enough is being done to insure the survival of our native dogwood.

"The white flowers are the source of the dogwood's popularity, yet the real value of the species lies in its fruit and its high calcium content," says Dan Lay, wildlife biologist for Texas Parks and Wildlife Department. Mr. Lay resides in Nacogdoches and is active in projects of the surrounding area. He goes on to say, "the dominant pine contribute acid to the forest soil and dogwood serves as a sweetner. Dogwood is the best source of calcium on the generally acid soils of eastern Texas. It contains five to ten times more than other plants growing on the same site. Its calcium content may exceed two percent . . . water percolation . . . is much more rapid under a dogwood than under a pine. Soil fertility, condition, organic matter, and water-holding capacity are enhanced by the dogwood."

"Deer browse the leaves and twigs and even consume the fallen, dried leaves. They eat the fruit from September to February. Turkeys eat the fresh fruits and scratch old stones out of leaf litter the year round. Squirrels eat the seed's germ in August (before it ripens)," says Mr. Lay, "and a variety of birds relish the fruit."

Where forestry is presently practiced with an eye toward maximum utilization for wood pulp purposes, many dogwoods are being destroyed. Burning, used in pine culture, is destructive to dogwood. Herbicides also claim their toll.

In the words of the song — "when spring is bustin' out all over" the flowering dogwood stands like a bride in shimmering white lace among the stately pines. But if our ancient Red Man should return, he would weep over the rape and slaughter of her humanoid trunks. In times past, they were arrayed in majesty that matched the fairness of his maidens and undergirded with strength of his warrior braves. How would he now know the time for planting maize (corn) without its flowering as an indicator that all danger of frost had passed? How would his children bleach their teeth without an abundance of twigs, or keep the gums healthy without application of the sap within? What would serve so well to cool his burning brow?

The Indian Chief, wise to the ways of nature, would surely cry out for his beloved dogwood. She is "the bride of the forest" and everybody's favorite among the dwindling forest trees of East Texas. If he followed the trail of fire or the song of the saw, he might turn out an epilogue that goes something like this:

> The bark is gone
> From the dogwood knot.
> The pines grow tall
> Where the blaze is hot.
> Wildlife starves
> And a share is dead;
> Man has no heart
> With his brilliant head.

References

Bailey, Liberty Hyde, The Standard Encyclopedia of Horticulture, New York, 1930.
Coon, Nelson, Using Plants for Healing, New York, 1963.
Coon, Nelson, Using Wayside Plants, New York, 1960.
Folsom-Dickerson, W. E. S., The White Path, San Antonio, 1965.
Hill, Albert F., Economic Botany, 1952.
Hohes, Pauline Buck, A Centennial History of Anderson County Texas, San Antonio, 1936.
Lay, Daniel, W., "Beauty Plus", Texas Parks and Wildlife, Vol. XXVI, no. 10 p 25
Massey, Mary Elizabeth, Erstaz in the Confederacy, Columbia, 1952.
Reeves, R. G. and D. C. Bain, Flora of South Central Texas, 1947.
Collier's Encyclopedia, 1967.

Dogwood Trails (Brochure), Palestine Chamber of Commerce.
Encyclopedia Americana, 1965.
The Dispensatory of the U.S., 25th Edition, 1947.
Tyler County Dogwood Festival (Brochure), Tyler County Chamber of Commerce, Woodville.
Interview with Troy Lewis, December 24, 1971.
Interview with Jane and Ray Nicholaides, January 10, 1972.

13

Historical Aspects of Linguistic Research in East Texas

by
Fred A. Tarpley

Fred A. Tarpley is Head of the Department of Literature and Languages at East Texas State University, Commerce, Texas. He is the author of **Place Names of Northeast Texas**, and has served as President of the East Texas Historical Association.

13

For the past several years, I have been asking East Texans what they call illegitimate children, the part of the day just before supper, worthless dogs, and food made from hogs' intestines.

Wherever I travel I make inquiry about epitaphs in local cemeteries and origins of such geographical names as Mud Dig, Poetry, Sweat Box, Scrouge Out, Elysian Fields, and Shake Rag. These questions are all part of grass roots research done by linguists who are interested in regional language patterns.

What the natives call illegitimate children, worthless dogs, and other lexical concepts will determine the local spoken dialect. How epitaphs have been composed and spelled on tombstones from one generation to the next will reflect the steady evolution of the written language. Origins of map names for towns, streams, hills, and streets will reveal significant information about pioneer family names, foreign language influence, natural features of the land, and word corruptions.

In each of these three fields of linguistic research — regional dialect, cemetary epitaphs, and geographical place names — I have been unable to confine my work or my interest strictly to the discipline of language study. Often I have trespassed with delight and reward into the domain of history, folklore, sociology, economics, geography, religion, architecture, psychology, and related fields.

The purpose of the following discussion is to outline certain historical aspects that cannot and should not be avoided when linguistic research is conducted in East Texas.

My first field of my linguistic research — regional dialect — resulted in a doctoral dissertation at Louisiana State University entitled **A Word Atlas of Northeast Texas**. For this study, I interviewed two hundred native informants in twenty-six counties in the northeast corner of Texas and recorded their answers to 127 dialect questions. This area covers the counties bounded on the north by Red River, the east by Arkansas and Louisiana, the west by a line halfway between Dallas and Fort Worth, and the south by an arbitrary line including Ellis, Kaufman, Van Zandt, Smith, Gregg, and Harrison counties.

A major chapter in the dialect study was devoted to a consideration of the people and historical background of Northeast Texas. The most valuable single volume written about the settlement of the area is an unpublished doctoral dissertation at the University of Texas by Rex W. Strickland, entitled **Anglo-American Activites in Northeastern Texas, 1803-45**.

The earliest recorded white settlement in Northeast Texas is reported by H. Yoakum in his **History of Texas**, published in 1856. According to Yoakum a trading-company under the direction of M. Francois Hervey came from Natchitoches, Louisiana, in 1750 to settle eventually in an ancient Caddo village on the Red River in what is now Red River County. Several French families prospered there, growing corn, tobacco, and garden vegetables. But in 1770 after Louisiana had passed into the hands of Spain and no attention was paid to the

French settlers on the upper Red River, the colony returned to the vicinity of Natchitoches to provide educational and social benefits for the children.

After 1770, Northeast Texas was left to roving Indian tribes and to white fugitives from justice. A spur of Trammel's Trace was laid out by horse thieves who needed a route to Nacogdoches to sell animals stolen in Missouri. In 1815 law-abiding settlers began to arrive at Pecan Point, near the buffalo crossing on the Red River in present-day Red River County. This important center of early settlement in Northeast Texas was the destination of many Southern mountaineers, whose boats carried them down the Cumberland River to its mouth, down the Ohio to the Mississippi, to the mouth of the Red River and then to Natchitoches and beyond.

For many years, inhabitants of the Red River settlements were perplexed by the anomalous legal status. They regarded themselves as citizens of the United States, and they were justified in this claim because of the ill-defined boundary line between Spanish Texas and the American territory of Arkansas. At the same time, had the area south of Red River actually been considered within the boundaries of the United States, the residents were encroaching upon unsurveyed public domain.

The Texas Revolution of 1836, strangely enough, secured the independence of Northeast Texas, not from Mexico, but from the United States. Had the battle of San Jacinto been lost, the Americans would almost certainly have held on to Miller County, Arkansas, but with San Jacinto won, westerners let the long disputed area between the Red River and the Sabine slip by default into the Republic of Texas.

A study of population sources also casts light on dialects in Northeast Texas. The states which sent early settlers into East Texas may be discovered in the tables of statistics prepared by Barnes F. Lathrop in his valuable study, **Migration into East Texas, 1835-1860**. It may be concluded from Mr. Lathrop's statistics, taken from ante-bellum census records, that the typical Northeast Texan came from English and Scotch-Irish stock, in greatest numbers from Southern mountain areas and in second greatest numbers from Southern plantation areas.

In the case of my study, the historian's reports on migrations were very helpful in suggesting the kinds of dialects that settlers would have brought into the area with them. When records of the former homes of immigrants are not available, the results of the dialect study can often lead the historian to a hypothesis regarding migrations by tracing the dialects found in an area to their geographical sources. Thus history and dialectology are closely allied.

In my **Word Atlas of Northeast Texas**, I was able to draw several major conclusions, some of them with historical implications:

The first conclusion is that the vocabulary within the region of Northeast Texas is highly homogeneous. Geographical factors are less important in word distribution than the age, sex, and education of the native speaker and the size of the community in which he lives.

Significant geographical distribution of Northeast Texas vocabulary is summarized in the following list:

1. Artificial watering place for livestock
    tank (western counties; among younger informants)
    pool (central counties)
    pond (eastern counties; especially southeastern area)
2. Insect with a double set of transparent wings seen flying over water
    dragon fly (standard educated usage)
    snake doctor
    mosquito hawk (eastern counties)
    skiter hawk (eastern counties)
3. Large sack made of burlap
    tow sack
    croker sack (southeastern counties)
4. Clavicle of chicken that children play a game with
    pulley bone
    wishbone (southeastern counties)
5. Milk that is beginning to turn sour
    blinky

        blue john (southeastern counties)
        blink john (Upshur County)
6. A small scarlet insect that bores into the skin
        chigger
        redbug (eastern counties)
7. Bird that makes holes in trees with its bill
        peckerwood, red head (eastern counties)
        woodpecker
8. Motherless calf
        maverick (western counties)
        orphan
9. Block of land in the center of a business district
        square
        plaza (Lamar County and adjoining area)
10. Little boy's weapon made of rubber strips on a forked stick
        sling shot or nigger shooter
        nigger flipper, bean flip (Red River County)
        nigger killer (eastern Hopkins County, western Titus County)

Second, both the vocabulary and pronunciation of Northeast Texans may be closely aligned with Southern mountain speech more than with any other dialect area in the Eastern United States.

Third, special patterns of vocabulary and pronunciation separate the southeastern corner of Northeast Texas from the rest of the region and indicate that Marion, Harrison, and adjoining counties have more Southern Plantation qualities than the other counties.

Fourth, not until linguistic atlases have been made available for all parts of the United States will the complete dialectal position of Northeast Texas be known.

My second field of linguistic research is cemetery epitaphs. Too often cemeteries are neglected archives for local history, legends, superstitions, and folkways. Egyptian pyramids, Roman tombs, and American Indian burial mounds have proved invaluable in interpreting past civilizations; but beyond the listing of foreboding Puritan epitaphs in New England and the compiling of genealogies, few serious studies have been made of cemeteries in the United States.

Cemeteries are equally important in linguistic and literary research. The changing language may be detected in the grammatical usage and spelling carved into tombstones by other generations. Graveyard poets find their inspiration in country churchyards amid the melancholy of what Thomas Gray's fine "Elegy" calls the "uncouth rhymes and shapeless sculpture." Epitaphs form a part of our literature, and epitaph-writing has become the literary domain of the artless masses as well as master poets. In older cemeteries, epitaphs preserve in stone the primary sources of folk fact and sentiment. In gestures of temporary immortality, chiseled letters spell out declarations of faith, love, and sorrow; favorite quotations; original verse; epigrams; and catalogs of terrestrial achievements and celestial goals. Cemetery architecture and burial customs mirror the artistic, social and religious patterns of the locality. Legends and superstitions that become the lore of the living are often originated and perpetuated in our communities of the dead.

Cemetery art recently became fashionable when a Ford Foundation grant was given two young artists who have transferred Early American stone sculpture from tombstones by rubbing a pencil over rice paper placed against the stone.

In East Texas, vague variations of a graveyard legend border between history and folk literature. Most tellings of the story agree that a woman sticks a sharp object — usually a knife — into a grave at night and in so doing catches her garment and dies of fright. At this point the similarities end. I first heard the story from my high school English teacher in Bowie County, who said she had been told of a girl in her hometown many years before who had pierced the edge of her apron while sticking her late boyfriend's favorite jack knife into his grave. According to the version handed down to some of my own students, a girl spending the night with a girl friend was dared to go to a nearby cemetery and stick a pitchfork into a fresh grave. One of the prongs caught her gown as she plunged the fork into the grave, and she died of fright.

The account given by Louise Hathcock in her book, **Legends of East Texas,** sets the story on a Colonel Stuart's plantation in southeastern Panola County during the Civil War. After the colonel's fourteen-year-old son died, the Negroes refused to plow within a half-mile radius of the cemetery where he was buried because they had seen ghosts hovering about his grave in the moonlight. The colonel offered a $5 goldpiece to Aunt Dorah, his late son's colored nurse, if she would take a butcher knife from her kitchen and drive it into the grave as proof she had visited the cemetery without fear during the night. When she was found dead at the grave the next morning, the colonel explained to the Negroes that she had probably driven the knife through her apron and trying to leave, thought a ghost was reaching for her from the grave. He said the ghost was only moonlight on the cobwebs.

Grammarians who take up epitaph reading are apt to be haunted by the gross errors they find carved permanently in stone. An English professor at East Texas State University is often tempted to red pencil the grammatical flaws on the tombstone of her great-grandparents. Their epitaph reads:

> Tis but the caskets that lies here
> The gems that filled them sparkles yet

What appears at first glance to be a mistake may actually be the historically standard usage for another generation. "Here lies the remains. . . ." gives a first impression of having an error in verb agreement, but consistent use of "remains" as a singular noun will be found in 19th century epitaphs, indicating this was considered correct usage at that time. Changes in spelling may also be observed, as in **council**, the spelling of a century ago for the word we now spell **counsel**.

Transient styles in Christian names may be reviewed in the epitaphs of different generations. Would any space-age East Texas parents dare give their offspring any of the following names of the past century: Temperance, Saphronia, Arminta, Cicero, Ucala, Narcissus, Ludie, Electra, Lular, Obediah, Singletary, or Edmonia?

A historical oddity in the Klondike community graveyard in Delta County is a tombstone facing westward. A local monument dealer recalls this is the grave of a man who killed his brother, was hanged, and denied the Christian tradition of being buried looking toward the east. This added punishment for condemned men seems to have been widespread.

The tradition, "Do not speak evil of the dead," is sometimes exaggerated in East Texas cemeteries. A striking example of kind words for the deceased may be seen at the grave of Bonnie Parker, the noted gun moll of Clyde Barrow during the 1930s. Their days of crime ended violently in an ambush in northern Louisiana. Friends laid Bonnie to rest near Dallas in Fishtrap Cemetery, a burial ground first used by citizens of LaReunion, a short-lived utopian colony of Frenchmen settled in **1855**. The gun moll's epitaph reads: "The life she lived will make this world better off."

When the owner of a grist mill died in Cooper, Texas, his family closed the business and used the mill stone to mark his grave.

Stories of lost cemeteries abound in Northeast Texas where some farmers still avoid plowing near groves of bois d'arc trees. According to tradition, bois d'arc trees were often planted as living fences encircling now forgotten graveyards.

In Southeast Texas and Southern Louisiana, tombstones frequently disappear as they sink into the soggy ground, but in East Texas, I discovered one that disappeared under other circumstances. A two-hour search for an original epitaph written by an eccentric citizen in a Northeast Texas town puzzled my guides who swore they had seen the stone not long before. The mystery of the missing monument was solved by the local marble dealer who remembered he had repossessed it and sandblasted the original verse after the family got behind in payments. This shrewd businessman outlined for me his trade-in plan, whereby old tombstones are accepted as down payments for new ones. He said the national trend in memorials is away from elaborate stones and epitaphs. "I used to put anything my customers wanted on the stones for free," he explained, "but some of 'em wanted the whole **Dallas News** put on, so I started charging fifty cents a letter, and that discouraged 'em."

In Farmersville is the grave of Sam Harris, known as the world's heaviest man, who weighed 691 pounds when he died of pneumonia in October, 1924, after swimming across a lake in Ballinger. One hundred miles east of Farmersville in Mt. Pleasant is the grave of Colonel Henry C. Thurston, whose height of 7 feet, 7½ inches gave him claim to the title of tallest man in the United States.

This sampling of my experiences growing out of epitaph collecting suggests the unclaimed wealth of history and folklore in the stone archives of East Texas cemeteries. A stroll through a graveyard or a chat with a caretaker in any part of the United States may introduce us to material available from no other source. The cemetery of the future, we are told, will bear the stamp of perpetually-endowed conformity and will be less colorful, but the cemetery of the past continues to be a neglected research center for linguists, historians, and folklorists.

My third field of linguistic interest in East Texas is geographical place names. From the types of names given may often be surmised the time of settlement and local characteristics of an earlier period.

With the help of students at East Texas State University, I have surveyed seventy-five Texas counties — most of them in East Texas — attempting to find the derivation of each geographical name. The basic list of names is taken from official county maps prepared by the Texas Highway Department.

The origins of East Texas place names may be conveniently sorted into nine categories, each of which reflects the history of the region.

In the first category are the names of people — either local citizens or non-local celebrities. Many local pioneer families, civic leaders, postmasters, railroad officials, ministers, and land developers have been honored by having places named for them.

In a second category are names referring to a geographic description of the countryside, its terrain, vegetation, minerals, animals or some other characteristic.

Some of the descriptions are objective as in Lone Oak, Caney Creek, Squash Hollow, Red Oak, Pecan Gap, Mesquite, Hick Grove, Sulphur Springs, East Mountain, and Dry Creek. Others are imaginatively subjective, as in Godly Prairie, Elysian Fields, Mount Joy, Good Springs, Mud Dig, Sweat Box, Paradise, and Mount Pleasant.

Names derived from nearby or distant places form a third category. Immigrants were especially fond of naming East Texas towns for former homes in other states or countries. You will find namesakes for Genoa, Italy, in Harris County; Kildare, Ireland, in Cass County; Manchester, England, in Red River County; Naples, Italy, in Morris County; Nome, Alaska, in Jefferson County; Paris, France, in Lamar County, and Malakoff, Russia, in Henderson County.

A fourth category of names may be traced to the Bible, literature, or to mythology, as in Zion, Macedonia, Ebenezer, Mars Hill, and Ivanhoe.

Names attributed to foreign language influence constitute a fifth group. American Indians provided Kiomatia, Kickapoo Creek, Caddo Mills, Lake Tawakoni, Cherokee County, and Chicota. From French came LaReunion; from Spanish came Golondrina Creek and Ladonia.

A sixth source of names is the blending of two or more words: Texarkana combines the names of three adjoining states. Mabank in Kaufman County takes Ma- from Dodge Mason and -bank from Tom Eubanks, both early settlers. Enon in Upshur County represents the first letter in the last names of four settlers, Eason, McNight, Olive, and Norris. Talco was derived from the name of the Texas, Arkansas and Louisiana Candy Co.

Backward spellings fall into a seventh group, with Reklaw (Walker spelled backwards) in Cherokee County and Sacul (Lucas spelled backwards) in Nacogdoches County.

Misunderstandings and misreadings — an eighth type of derivation — are exemplified by Bogata in Red River County and Warsaw in Kaufman County. Bogata was named for Bogota, Colombia, but the fancy penmanship in the application to the postal department was interpreted as Bogata. The spelling remained Bogata, the pronunciation Bogota.

White men in Kaufman County heard Indians talking about a place, calling it what sounded like Warsaw, when the Indians were trying to pronounce **water**.

In the ninth and most fascinating group of name derivations are those related to events or anecdotes.

Jot 'em Down in Delta County was a name a traveling salesman — who was a Lum and Abner fan — gave to a community where a new general store was being built.

Scrouge Out in Fannin County was a name given first to a school then to the surrounding rural community because students who did not arrive early at school had to scrouge out a seat on the benches.

Razor in Lamar County was named for a popular brand of tobacco.

Alba in Wood County and Snow Hill in Morris County are names referring to the color white, because the communities were intended for whites only.

Redwater in Bowie County was first called Ingersoll, after the famous atheist, because there were so many ungodly people there. The residents of Ingersoll did not object to the name until they got religion during a great revival during the 1880s. Then they changed the name to Redwater, referring to the red clay coloring of the water.

Coffeeville in Upshur County was a name which originated when the Civil War produced a scarcity of coffee. Settlers began to use parched corn, okra and other substitutes. A merchant from this area went to Jefferson and brought back a supply of green coffee. Folks from miles around came to his store in the community, which became known as Coffeeville.

Ginger in Kaufman County was first named Spicer for the Spicer Tie Yard, but railroad officials were afraid of confusing the post office and the spur track stop. "If you insist on a spicy name," a Katy railroad official said, "why don't you name the place Ginger?" So they did.

Also in Kaufman County is Poetry, which was named not by a poet but by a stranger, for a malnourished dog he called poor Tray.

Hog Eye in Gregg County was named for a hog thief who had a good eye for pigs.

Into a tenth category must fall many names whose origins are unknown. Some of the explanations have been lost forever; others are yet to be found in county histories, newspapers, memoirs, or in interviews with oldtimers.

Sometimes more than one explanation will be given. Some folks in Shake Rag, a nickname for Pleasant Grove in Rusk County, say Shake Rag originated because wives signaled to their husbands to come to dinner by shaking an apron. Others say a teacher threatened to spank a student so hard he wouldn't have anything but rags to shake.

Of tremendous influence in providing and inspiring East Texas place names was the railroad, for wherever the railroad stopped, a new name was needed. The U. S. Postal Department also had a far reaching effect on name giving, because applications for post office names were rejected if another Texas town had already been given the same name.

In each of the categories of place name origins — as well as in investigations of cemetery epitaphs and regional dialect — the linguist will encounter fascinating segments of East Texas history.

14

The World's Champion Fiddler's Festival at Crockett: An East Texas Tradition

by
Joe Angle

Marvin J. Angle is a native of Marshall, Texas but attended school in Nacogdoches. He presently practices law in Jacksonville, Texas.

14

Every year in the small East Texas town of Crockett fiddlers from around the state and nation gather at the Davy Crockett Memorial Park. Here the most skillful fiddler present is chosen. The winner is something more than the best performer present for this musician also carries the title of World's Champion Fiddler. However, a description of this contest is incomplete if it stops with only the fiddler. For those attending, it is a social event of great significance.

On the northeast side of the semicircle of parked cars and pickups is located the pavilion (a euphemism for a large, tin roofed shed), under which the contest is held. Here people gather to hear the music they have grown up with, meet their friends, get in some gossip, and judge fiddlers. Almost everyone considers himself a judge of fiddlers. In front of the pavilion, under a large shade tree, sits a wooden barrel full of water, with the name of the local funeral home printed on its side. On the south side are concession stands operated by the Festival's sponsoring organization, Beta Sigma Phi. Also on this side is the registration table, shaded by a tent with Waller Funeral Home also printed on it. A bit further east, is a group of chairs in which the contestants sit to await their chance at the prize money.

About seventy-five yards to the east of this area is a row of trees that follows the road that winds through the park. Under the shade of these trees cars are parked, and around these cars groups of fiddlers and guitar players gather for impromptu jam-sessions. About four or five fiddlers and a couple of guitar players usually make up one of these groups. They agree upon one song and play it in its traditional key. Each takes his turn and plays until he is finished with his version or until one of the others in the group takes up the lead. When each has had his turn, they stop and chat a while before beginning another song. This is not indigeneous to Crockett, because it happens at all fiddling contests.[1] This gives the fiddler a chance to hear and size-up his opponents and try to judge what kind of day he will have. This idea of the "good day" is quite strong among the old-time fiddlers. There are so many fiddlers of near equal skill that this plays a prominent part among the contestants in justifying the choice of the winner.[2]

These informal sessions also provide an opportunity to get in all the fiddle playing desired. If the fiddler relied solely on his performance, that would mean only about five minutes of playing time. But, perhaps the most important function of the session is that it is a chance for the fiddler to meet and visit with old friends. There is a strong spirit of camaraderie among fiddlers, and a large percentage of them know each other. They share in a unique talent and attend some of the same contests, like those at Gilmer, Hurst, Athens, Pasadena, or Yoakum. Close relationships are usually cemented at these gatherings.

Roy Garner, a perennial master of ceremonies of the Crockett Festival, took a group of past champions to Hemisfair to perform. Every night after their performance they would gather at their motel and play until the early hours of the morning. When the group broke up

Sunday night Garner went back to Crockett, but E. J. Hopkins and some other fiddlers gathered again at the motel. They played until early Monday morning. Hopkins than drove from San Antonio to Houston to start work that same morning as a city policeman.[3]

It is also under these trees at Crockett that picnic lunches are eaten from the trunks of cars or off the tailgates of pickups. This is also the place where the observers and the participants drink beer, which is theoretically forbidden. Most people sit under the pavilion, but a large number of them mill around over the grounds. There are people sitting under trees, people at the concession stands, kids playing chase, and scattered about are occasional pallets on which perspiring children and adults are lying.

These contests have not always been as they are in Crockett. At earlier rural community gatherings among the events scheduled would be a fiddlers contest. Frequently, they were quite informal and only concerned one community or one county.

Fiddlers would occasionally meet without the benefit of an official contest to find out who was "give up" as the best fiddler.[4] If it was not a contest, perhaps it was just a chance for fiddlers to get together or to play for a box supper or ice cream social. In Crockett, there had been "get-togethers" of fiddlers at the north end of town or at the home of V. B. Tunstall some years before the beginning of the fiddler's festival.[5] In Athens, Texas, a similar contest grew out of a farmer's study course in 1932.[6]

The date and location of the first formal contest is in doubt. Both Texas fiddlers and those from the southeast claim that distinction. While no date can be agreed upon, most people put it sometime around the turn of the century.[7] One contest, the annual Atlanta, Georgia, Old Fiddler's Convention, presumably began as early as the 1880s.[8]

By the 1920s, notices in newspapers began to appear.[9] It was in 1925 that Stephen Vincent Benet published his "The Mountain Whippoorwill or How Hillbilly Jim Won the Great Fiddler's Prize." Gid Tanner of the popular "Skillet Lickers" appeared frequently at fiddlers conventions around the Atlanta, Georgia, area from the early 1900s into the 1920s. Most of the contests were local because of the difficulty of travel.

The guiding light for the Crockett Fiddlers Festival was V. B. Tunstall, Sr., known in the area as "Barker." Barker Tunstall was the eighteenth child of a family of nineteen (his father married again after his first wife died and lived to be ninety-nine). Tunstall, from an early age, had been interested in music. He first studied music at the age of six under a certain Mr. Mayer, who opened an opera house in Crockett. Even though Barker Tunstall received this formal training and liked classical music, he also remained very fond of the old fiddle tunes. He ended up making his living quite close to music. When he was about twenty, he travelled to Galveston, where he studied piano tuning. He travelled about over the countryside on horseback or on a bicycle, tuning pianos. He was never a man to let business interfere too strongly with one of his great loves, music. While he went about his work, he carried his violin and when he got the chance he would have a "set-to" with one of his customers or with one of the families along his way, playing the old fiddle songs or perhaps a bit of more recent music that often came in sheet music form.[10]

Tunstall was also the man one contacted on matters concerning music in the Houston County area. Besides tuning pianos and doing some barbering, he taught music (mainly strings) in several towns in the area, such as Corrigan and Trinity. In a time when people were entertained by less sophisticated media than today, Tunstall provided entertainment with the assistance of his ten children. He divided them into two troops and travelled about the area performing variety shows for different groups. If someone needed musical entertainment for a cotton festival or a fiddler for a fair or dance, he sought out Barker Tunstall for the arrangements.[11] He also amused his friends with the construction of musical instruments out of common tools and appliances like rakes and shovels or water filled jars.[12]

It was the musical man who was to lead in the establishment of an annual event known as the World's Champion Fiddlers' Festival. In fact, his name became so closely connected with the contest that it was often referred to as "Barker Tunstall's Old Fiddler's Festival,"[13] and after he died, succeeding contests were dedicated in his memory.[14]

One day in 1937, Tunstall, along with Terry VanPelt, Raymond Cornelius, W. E. Keeland, and Homer Galloway, gathered in Cornelius's hotel. They believed that the old fiddling tunes of their fathers were in danger of becoming extinct, so they made preliminary plans for a fiddler's festival to be held in Crockett. It was to be patterned after one held in Athens.[15] However, the festival was to be more than simply a plan for preservation. It was to be a day of fun for those who listened as well as those who played. The men formed committees which took care of the arrangements of publicity, fund raising, and the securing of facilities. The committees' personnel changed from time to time until they became defunct when the festival in the late 1940s was taken over by the Jaycees. The committee had included such people as Bob Greene, H. V. Trube, Eliza Bishop, Hattie Bell Milburn, and Roy Garner.[16]

The publicity, such as there was, was handled by Tunstall. During the course of his years in the music business he had come to know quite a number of fiddlers in the area. In order to spread the word, he began writing the fiddlers he knew, telling them of the new contest. As things progressed and the operation of the contest changed hands, letters were still sent out and notices appeared in local newspapers, but one rather clever device was added. Tunstall, who was also an amateur poet, began to publish poems with fiddling and contest themes in the local newspaper. For example:

    Old Dan Tucker is coming to town
    To swing those pirty gals round and round,
    The Arkansas traveler will be here too.
    So will that sweet little Sioux City Sue
    Little Annie Rooney and her ma and pa
    Will be right here to dance Turkey in the Straw;

>So tune up your fiddle and rodin your bow
>And we'll all crack down on Cotton-Eyed Joe.
>
>I love my apples and I love my plums puddin'
>I love Ida Red and I love Sally Goodin'
>Another old tune I love to hear them saw
>Is that old tune they call "Turkey in the Straw."
>
>Now be sure not to miss this wonderful treat,
>'Cause ther's many old friends you would love to meet,
>So gather up your instruments and get them all in tune;
>And meet me at the fair park the 28th day of June.
>   (1946)[17]

Also:

>It's time to get your fiddle out and rosin up that bow
>That fiddlin' day will soon be here and we are rarin' to go
>We'll tell you more about it as we plan and time draws near
>For it's going to be the biggest in this grand old state this
>   year.
>
>For the merchants who cooperate have never let us down
>And that's what keeps us rollin' as the years keep rolling
>   'round
>While Congress and our leaders are doing lots of piddling
>We'll just tune up our old gords and do a lot of fiddling.
>
>The J. C. boys will be right there to make this
>   day one grand affair.
>All set up and ready to go when them boys start draggin'
>   the bow
>And when them fiddlers begin to play watch them dancers
>   rock and sway
>Here's that man that does the calling, listen to those babies
>   squalling.
>
>So don't forget the 8th of June and meet me at the park
>You'll hear some good old fiddlin' all day long after dark
>And all of you who come each year I am sure you under-
>   stand
>We'll have the girls from Goree Farm and that prison band.
>   (1951)[18]

Perhaps the compsitions were not exactly in the style of an Ezra Pound, but they did reflect something of the attitude and outlook of the local citizenry toward the festival. For all its faults, Tunstall's poetry does a better job of bringing out the flavor of a contest than did

Stephen Vincent Benet in "The Mountain Whippoor-will. . . ."

Other devices for publicity that were and are still being used are handbills, street banners and, since Beta Sigma Phi took over the sponsorship of the festival, television.

The money for the prizes came from the donations made by local merchants. At first, the prizes were meager, no doubt reflecting the hard times of the thirties. The top prizes were $50 and $25 and the lesser prizes were various types of "kind," such as a box of cigars or a basket of groceries.[19] As times became better, so did the prizes. Later, the "kind" was dropped and only cash prizes were given, with the prize money reaching several hundreds of dollars. There was an exception in 1957 when a fiddle was given as a prize.

At first, Mr. Tunstall also arranged for the judges who usually came from surrounding towns.[20] Tunstall's successor to obtain judges was a past champion fiddler, Jesse Johnson, who had been taught fiddling by Tunstall.[21] At the present time, Johnson is still in charge of the selection of judges.

In the early days of the festival the fiddlers were judged on the tune, i.e., its difficulty and the manner in which it was played; harmony (the harmony produced by double stopping or bowing two strings at once); and audience reception. This applied to both the individual fiddler and the band. It soon became evident that this method led to the "crowd pleaser" "beating out" the really fine fiddler merely on the basis of his audience appeal. So, in 1954, this was changed and for a number of years the contest was conducted on a kind of double standard. There was one set of standards for the individual fiddler and one set (the old set) for the fiddler bands. Things continued in this light until 1961 when the fiddle band contest was dropped.[23]

The new manner of judging started off by giving every fiddler twenty-five points in four categories, (tune, timing, bowing, and fingering) for a total of one hundred points. From this, the judges would begin to deduct points for mistakes they observed. The bow must be held correctly and be properly tilted, and the little finger must be kept folded in. If the little finger sticks out, it is called "letting the finger sail or fly." Notes must be made with the proper finger and the bottom of the hand must be kept off the neck of the fiddle. The tune must be played in its original key and be of some degree of difficulty, and the tempo must be steady with no rushing or dragging of the beat.[23] The three judges sit in the audience with a score sheet and observe and listen to each fiddler. They then tally up his score.

The method of judging used in Crockett does have its critics. There has been some pressure for them to adopt the rules set down by a rather interesting organization called the "Federation of Old Time Fiddling Judges."[24] Their criteria for judging are authenticity, rhythm and timing, tonal quality, and clarity.[25] Notice that all these criteria do not involve looking at the fiddler. It is for this reason that frequently contests which go by these rules have their judges separated from the audience in compartments sealed off from all sound except that of the contestant. These judges identify the fiddler by number only. This way, they feel there can be no chance for favoritism. The feeling in Crockett is that there has to be some kind of barrier that separates the men from the boys. It is for this reason there are sections on fingering and bowing and the judges sit in the audience to observe the contestants.

There are some insurances against the failings of human nature. The judges for the fiddler's festival go through a screening period of about three years. Their competence in playing the fiddle is determined; the opinion of others as to his honesty is checked and his conduct at other contests is observed. The individual is then put on a waiting list to await his chance at being a judge.[26] This is quite different from the days when Barker Tunstall would simply pick the judges for the contest from among his acquaintances.

The contest is divided into three age categories: 75 years and up, 50 to 75, and 50 and under (one year there was a 20 and under group). Each group plays separately, with each fiddler playing two songs, aided by one accompanist. The songs that are played must be traditional (a very elastic term) and there must be no singing or trick fiddling, i.e., playing the fiddle behind the back or between the legs. A first, second, and third place winner for these nine to determine the winner of the festival. The winner of the festival then meets the previous World's Champion to determine the World's Champion for that year. At this step, each play-off contestant must play a breakdown, a rag, a polka, a waltz, and a tune of his choice. The World's Champion, besides getting prize money, has his name engraved on the large festival trophy, and he keeps a "traveling trophy" until the next year when he returns to defend his title. If he wins three times in a row, he keeps the traveling trophy and is retired from competition.[37]

In 1948 when the Jaycees took over the contest from the committee the title World's Champion Fiddler's Festival was recorded with the Texas Secretary of State in Austin and with a fiddler's association in Tennessee.[28] In the early fifties an attempt was made on the part of a contest also located in Tennessee to use the title, World's Champion. Court procedures were begun and attorneys for the Crockett Jaycees presented Crockett's case and won. The result was that in effect a copyright on the title was gained.[29]

At the beginning the contest was held on the east side of the courthouse which occupied the town square. The program began about 10:00 a.m. At this time the stage was left open to anyone who wished to perform. At noon the fiddlers were given a barbecue dinner in the space behind the local hotel.[30] In those days emphasis was placed principally on the fiddle band (a fiddle, one or two guitars, a bass fiddle, etc.) rather than on the individual fiddler. Prizes for both the best band and the best fiddler were given. However, the emphasis on the band shifted toward the individual fiddler until 1961 when the band was dropped. In the evening after the winner had been selected the east end of the square was roped off and a dance followed.[31] The music was provided either by the fiddlers themselves or by some group hired for the occasion.

After World War II the festival was moved to the city park, much to the delight of the local businessmen who found it had caused a hopeless traffic snarl. The festival was held on the west side of the park with the fiddlers performing on a raised open platform. The platform still stands but is not used because as the festival began to grow it became necessary to build a new pavilion. This was built in 1955 and is still in use.[32]

After the first early experiment there has always been a musical group from the state prison system to provide entertainment in the morning or between divisions of fiddlers.[33] Two of the most popular of these groups have been the "Goree Girls" from the Goree Farm and the Eastham Farm Prison Swingsters. It is not really clear whether it is their talent or the fact that they are prisoners that accounts for their popularity. One of the greatest successes of the day in 1968 was when one of the singers from the prison sang a plaintive country and western ballad entitled "Please Release Me." Like Prison rodeos, the invitations to the singers carries a message that they are not forgotten and the maintenance of a sense of humor is a healthy sign.

The "outside" entertainment, however, has included something more than what the prison system was able to provide. Most of the time the committee or whoever happens to be the sponsor manages to book the appearance of some well known "county and western" artist or group to play for the dance after the contest and to provide entertainment during the day. This type of music has always been popular in the rural South and East Texas is no exception. A great favorite was the Lightcrust Doughboys who provided the music for "Pappy Pass the Biscuits" W. Lee O'Daniel during his campaign for governor of Texas. Houston County was carried handily by O'Daniel, which perhaps goes a long way in explaining the Light Crust Doughboys' popularity.[34] The story is that these men had been employees of a flour mill and enjoyed playing together during their time off so much that they made their hobby their work.[35] O'Daniel was a flour salesman and when he campaigned his children passed small flour barrels through the crowd into which the crowd was asked to drop coins or bills to help finance the campaign.

The more popular the "outside" group, of course, the more attendance there is at the dance. A good example is the crowd that attended in 1954 when Bob Wills and the Texas Playboys were the featured attraction. Wills is perhaps the best known as a pioneer of "Western Swing" and in the 1940s had great success with his recording of "San Antonio Rose." To the average urbanized American this means nothing or at best it is a cue to smile or laugh knowingly but to "country and western" fans, which includes a big slice of East Texas citizenry, it is serious business and Bob Wills and performers like him are "somebody."[36] This particular evening he enjoyed the distinction of having the greatest attendance at a festival dance. This is very important to the contest. The proceeds from the dance go to help defray the costs of the festival, and while the day is devoted to the fiddler, the dance is pushed for this reason.[37]

There have been other attractions at the festival beside the fiddle players themselves and recording artists. For a fews hours, (1952 and 1955) the cowboy film star, "Montana 'Monte' Hale," made his appearance to dutifully sign autographs, give shooting demonstrations, and be a judge (1952).[38] For a number of years square dancing and square dance calling contests were held. There have also been visits by the Alabama-Coushatta Indians. They entertained the crowds with their dancing and by just generally being Indians. In 1951, there was one special occasion for the Indians and Robert John Baldwin, the grandson of one of the founders of the fiddling contest, Terry VanPelt. On this occasion the young boy of two years was "adopted" into the Indian tribe.[39] He was chosen for this honor because he was a direct descendent of Sam Houston and the Alabama-Coushattas wished to pay tribute to a man they had respected for his honest dealings with them. The lad was given the name of "Yellow Pine" and was admonished by the chief's son, Haskell Sylestine, to "be as the pine tree, friend to both rich and poor through the years."[40]

There were also other attractions. In the late 1940s and early 1950s a beauty contest was conducted under the direction of Miss Eliza Bishop, who for many years had acted as secretary to the festival's organizational committee. Girls from Crockett and the surrounding communities between the ages of sixteen and twenty vied for the honor of being queen of the festival.[41] During the Davy Crockett craze of the 1950s, a contest for boys under thirteen years was sponsored by the White Cross Surgical Dressing Company in conjunction with the introduction of their new "Davy Crockett First Aid Kit." The winner received fifty dollars and a trip to Ft. Worth to view the movie Davy Crockett with its star, Fess Parker.[42] In 1961 and 1962, there were fly-ins to the Houston County Airport. A complimentary breakfast and transportation to the contest was provided to the participants by the Crockett Community Council.[43]

If someone were to declare the festival silly and provincial, the people of Houston County could care less. It is their festival and they will schedule and provide things that lie within their resources and their tastes. They are not accountable to anyone else. The music they gather to listen to represents for many a pleasant relief from the sounds of the modern man and his mass culture. For some, it is a symbol of rebellion against the age, a symbol of individualism. It is not the rootless and anarchic individualism so much in vogue, for it has not divorced itself from its past. It stands proud with a firm foundation in tradition. But for others the music is simply a part of life. That is the difference between "being" and "observing."

Manifestations of an "agrarian myth?" Maybe. But even if it is, there is a certain amount of value and truth to some myths, and whatever its qualities it is certainly one that is believed by a great number of people. For proof all one has to do is tune to a country and western radio station and count the songs which, for all practial purposes, sing the praises of a return to a simpler life with traditional values. The modern fiddle contest has its message. In its way it also sings the praises of another way of life.

Notes

1. Charles Farot. "Texas Fiddle Favorites," County Record No. 707.
2. Letter from E. J. Hopkins, dated Houston, April 15, 1968. In possession of writer.
3. Roy Garner, personal interview with the writer, Crockett, Texas, April 18, 1968.
4. Josiah H. Combs, The Folksongs of the Southern United States (Folksongs, De Medi Des Etas Unis) D. K. Wilgus (ed.), (Austin, 1967), 91.
5. Roy Garner, personal interview with the writer, Crockett, Texas, April 15, 1968.
6. V. B. Tunstall, Jr., personal interview with the writer, Crockett, Texas, April 15, 1968.
7. Charles Farot, "Virginia Breakdown," County Record No. 705.
8. Guthrie T. Meade, "Fiddler's Contests and Conventions," program of the Smithsonian Annual Festival of American Folklife, 1968, 33; For a discussion of Henry Ford's influence on fiddling contests see John Greenway, "Country and Western: the Music of America," The American West, V (November, 1968), 35-36.
9. Farot. "Virginia Breakdown."
10. V. B. Tunstall, Jr., personal interview with the writer, Crockett, Texas, April 15, 1968.
11. Ibid.
12. Raymond E. Cornelius, personal interview with the writer, Crockett, Texas, April 12, 1968.
13. Crockett (Texas) Courier, June 3, 1948.
14. Crockett (Texas) Courier, June 18, 1953.
15. V. B. Tunstall, Jr., personal interview with the writer, Crockett, Texas, April 15, 1968.
16. Raymond E. Cornelius, personal interview with the writer, Crockett, Texas, April 12, 1968.
17. Crockett (Texas) Courier, June 13, 1946.
18. Crockett (Texas) Courier, May 17, 1951.
19. Raymond E. Cornelius, personal interview with the writer, April 12, 1968.
20. Ibid.
21. V. B. Tunstall, Jr., personal interview with the writer, Crockett, Texas, April 15, 1968.
22. Roy Garner, personal interview with the writer, September 21, 1968.
23. Jesse Johnson, personal interview with the writer, April 15, 1968.
24. Roy Garner, personal interview with the writer, September 21, 1968.
25. Kelly Kirksey, "The Fiddling Contest Judges," 2-4, MSS in personal possession.

26. Roy Garner, personal interview with the writer, September 21, 1968.

27. Roy Garner, personal interview with the writer, April 18, 1968.

28. Houston County Courier, April 29, 1965.

29. Letter from Roy Garner to the writer, dated, Crockett, Texas, June 22, 1968.

30. Raymond E. Cornelius, personal interview with the writer, April 12, 1968.

31. Roy Garner, Crockett, Texas, letter, June 22, 1968, to the writer.

32. Ibid.

33. Raymond E. Cornelius, personal interview with the writer, April 12, 1968.

34. **Texas Almanac and State Industrial Guide 1939-1940** (Dallas, 1940), 360.

35. Crockett (Texas) Courier, May 29, 1952.

36. This is reflected by the fact that country and Western music brings sixty million dollars a year into the city of Nashville. Nashville has ten recording studios, twenty-six record companies, 265 music publishers and over 1,000 union musicians. Charles Portis, "The New Sound from Nashville," **The Saturday Evening Post**, 238 (February 12, 1965), p. 31.

37. Mrs. Jo Harkins, personal interview with the writer, Crockett, Texas, June 14, 1968.

38. Crockett (Texas) Courier, May 19, 1952.

39. Crockett (Texas) Courier, June 14, 1951.

40. Terry VanPelt, Personal interview with the writer, Crockett, Texas, April 15, 1968.

41. Crockett (Texas) Courier, May 25, 1950.

42. Crockett (Texas) Courier, June 9, 1955.

43. Houston County Courier, June 15, 1961.